Closing the Chart

Photo courtesy Beth Corbin-Hsi

"What set Dr. Hsi apart from other doctors was his deep concern for those in his care and his ability to listen and empathize, no matter how long it took. In doing so he restored the human element to the practice of medicine. I truly believe that he practiced medicine in a state of grace."

—Marian Nygren, Patient

Closing the Chart

A Dying Physician Examines
Family, Faith and Medicine

Steven D. Hsi, M.D.
WITH
Jim Belshaw
AND
Beth Corbin-Hsi

UNIVERSITY OF NEW MEXICO PRESS | ALBUQUERQUE

Library of Congress Cataloging-in-Publication Data

Hsi, Steven D.

  A dying physician examines family, faith, and medicine /
Steven D. Hsi, with Jim Belshaw and Beth Corbin-Hsi.— 1st ed.

      p. ; cm.

  ISBN 0-8263-3038-x (paper : alk. paper)

  1. Hsi, Steven D.—Health.   2. Patients—Psychology.

3. Physicians—Biography.   4. Physician and patient—Anecdotes.

[DNLM: 1. Hsi, Steven D.   2. Patients—psychology—Personal Narratives.

3. Takayasu's Arteritis—psychology—Personal Narratives.   4. Physician-

Patient Relations—Personal Narratives.   5. Physicians—psychology—

Personal Narratives.   WZ 100 H874d 2004]

I. Belshaw, Jim, 1944–   II. Corbin-Hsi, Beth, 1948–   III. Title.

R726.5.H75 2004

610'.92—dc22

                    2003022128

Design and composition by Melissa Tandysh

In 1997, my friend and physician, Dr. Steven Hsi (pronounced "she") and I talked about writing a book. I had written two columns in the *Albuquerque Journal* on his experience as a patient with a life-threatening disease and its effect on his view of how medicine is taught and practiced.

"It changed my perspective as a doctor," he said then. "Being a patient with a serious, major illness forced me to confront issues that all patients must confront, issues that potentially could kill them. Realizing that you could go into surgery and not come out of it alive, realizing that you may never see your family and friends again changes you."

He began his education as a patient at Presbyterian Hospital in Albuquerque, New Mexico where he practiced medicine and where he underwent his first heart surgery in the summer of 1995. He learned more lessons in a second heart surgery eighteen months later at a California Medical Center, where he would become a heart valve "redo," an oft-repeated designation leading him to conclude that like so many patients before him he was viewed largely as human equipment to be repaired and sent on its way. The lessons would be highlighted again in October 1997, in a third heart surgery, this one also at the Medical Center. He came away thinking he had been in the hands of skilled mechanics who showed little interest in him beyond his status as a "redo."

I suggested Steve give some thought to writing a book. It seemed to me a good story with numerous points of reference along the way for him to examine the experience and how it changed him. Eventually, we decided to work on the project together. But the going was slow. The surgeries and vagaries of the disease sapped his energy. When he was feeling well, he spent as much time as he could with his wife, Beth, and his sons, Andy and David.

Steve often spoke of the difference between a physician and a healer. He felt strongly that healers had to be part of the community they served, not isolated from it, regardless of who erected the barriers, patients or the doctors themselves. He believed a healer had to deal with all of the patient's life—family, spiritual, medical.

This book is Steve's journey, a personal, detailed look at what serious disease does to the whole patient—the stresses that bring crushing pressure not only to the patient but to everyone close to him; the denial that even a well-trained medical professional must somehow hurdle; the debilitating irony of a man watching close friends come to help and feeling blessed to have such people around him but at the same time seeing only his own inadequacies because he cannot function without the help; the newfound clarity and focus with which he values each moment spent with his family; the unwavering religious faith that he returns to time and again because it brings strength and renewal.

"We take so much for granted in medicine," he said. "Someone comes in and we say, 'Well, you have this problem and we'll prescribe this medication.' In a scientific sort of way, we have this fix-it attitude. We might explain the potential side effects, but unless you've experienced it personally, you really don't know what kind of impact it will have on a patient's life. It's an abstraction. Patients want someone to care about them. Yes, they want us to treat them properly and do the right operation and give the right medicine—but underlying all that, they want somebody to care."

Steve died on March 25, 1999. He was 44 years old.

Jim Belshaw
Albuquerque, New Mexico

Notes
Third Heart Surgery
Medical Center
10/26/97

*Day before discharge. New valve. Good news. No inflammation.
Out of ICU. Long day. Anti-coagulating process begun. Heparin to
thin blood. Doses increasing. I'm beginning to be concerned.*

*Told Beth to leave early (around 9 P.M.) She'd been staying late
every night. She went to friend's apartment.*

*Drifting off to sleep, felt something trickling down my arm.
Thought I was dreaming. Tried to sleep. Woke up. Blood flowing
from old IV puncture site on arm. Blood pooling in bed, soaking
into sheets. Survey rest of body. Bleeding from old wounds—PICC
line sticks, IV holes, surgical incisions. Everything bleeding.*

*Push call button for nurse. No response. Push again and again.
No response.*

*Fear: If I'm bleeding like this on the outside, what's happen-
ing on the inside?*

*Call Beth at apartment. She dials nurses' station in hospital.
Tells them patient is bleeding spontaneously and to get someone
to me immediately. Beth runs two blocks from apartment to
Medical Center.*

Consider: Patient's wife calling from outside hospital to tell nurses patient down the hall is in trouble. Incredible.

Nurse comes. Changing dressings when Beth arrives. Blood and serous fluid all over the bed.

Lab reports for 5:30 P.M. AAPT to measure specific clotting mechanism. Reference range 24.2-37.8. Goal for heparin patients 1.5 greater. Should be about 55 seconds. Mine logged at 180.0 seconds. "Panic value." Probably higher later that night. No doctor ever came to my room.

CHAPTER ONE

Jackie Chan's name will not be found in my medical chart. I have not seen my chart in its entirety and I can only guess at its size, but I am confident it is fat, that it bulges with all the appropriate facts of my history. I am certain Jackie Chan will not be in it. There will be no entry noting ten seconds spent with a movie star in a bookstore. There will be only dispassionate notes from well-trained medical professionals conducting themselves as they have been trained to conduct themselves.

I had undergone three heart surgeries in two years, numerous tests, dozens of visits to doctors' offices, extended stays in hospitals and long recuperative periods at home. I was 43 years old, a successful physician, married to a wonderful woman and blessed with two fine sons—all of it assaulted by a rare heart disease of such catastrophic power that it did more than threaten my life. It nearly destroyed my family.

It turned me inward, consuming me with doubt and anger and self pity. I am a competitive man, a lifelong athlete; I am unafraid of rigorous challenge, physical or intellectual. But the disease became an opponent like no other I'd known. It made demands I had not encountered nor imagined. For years, I engaged in a perilous denial that would have resulted in a finger-wagging lecture from me had I seen such behavior in one of my patients. When denial finally crumbled and treatment began, medicines flowed into my body that changed me physically and

3

psychologically until I raged at the most inconsequential acts of my children or imagined slights by my wife.

Outwardly, we coped, admired by our friends as we projected an image of strength and resolve in the face of crisis. Inside our home, bitterness consumed us. We wondered if we would survive.

"If only someone would have asked . . .," Beth and I would say later.

But no one did, least of all the many physicians with whom I came into contact. Regardless of the considerable compassion and caring of many of them, no one asked the questions that needed to be asked. I have come to believe this oversight was the single most grievous mistake my doctors made and one that eventually changed the way I approached patients in my own practice.

Like Jackie Chan, the unasked questions do not appear in my medical record. Nor is there any mention of my youngest son, David, who celebrated his tenth birthday on the day we waited in a bookstore for an audience with a movie star. For two hours we inched along in a line that began on the ground floor and snaked up to the fourth floor of the San Francisco Borders bookstore. I remember those hours vividly. I remember David's determined stoicism and nervous energy, his excitement and unabashed joy at the thought of being so close to greatness. I remember watching him and being aware that I was doing so. I remember feeling grateful that I could do it.

Such moments had become part of my healing. Like so many others before me, I had brushed against death too often not to come away with a new awareness of life. Two hours with David spent waiting for thirty seconds with a movie star carried as much restorative weight as anything that might be found in my medical chart. But there is no place for David or a movie star in my chart, no way to measure their worth, no impartial, precise manner by which to judge their effect. Even if there were, I doubt that many doctors would feel comfortable raising the subject of a movie star's spiritual worth or a son's medical efficacy, let alone scribble such an entry in my chart.

A chief resident's name will appear in it somewhere, however, no doubt in connection with a recalcitrant, uncooperative patient.

In January, 1997, after I was admitted to a major Medical Center in California for my second heart surgery, I wanted to speak to the surgeon into whose hands I would place my life. Earlier in the day, I had violated hospital convention by refusing to sign the surgical consent form before seeing him, an infringement upon protocol that had not endeared me to the chief resident. Around nine o'clock on the evening before my surgery, the surgeon, a renowned heart specialist, came into my room. Typical of large teaching institutions, a clutch of assistant surgeons and residents trailed behind him. When he approached my bed, the other doctors receded into the background.

As he explained what he was going to do, I began to feel intimidated and overwhelmed. As a fellow physician I should have been able to speak with him as a colleague, even though I was unfamiliar with this type of surgery. Instead, I found myself feeling much the patient, trying to understand but forgetting what I had so carefully planned to ask. Even my wife, Beth, an experienced nurse, and my brother, Andy, a pediatrician, remained silent in the presence of the formidable doctor.

I did not want to be just another piece of machinery to be fixed and sent on its way. Hoping for assistance, I glanced around the room at the other doctors. They leaned against the walls, avoiding eye contact with me. They looked at the floor, they took notes, they feigned interest in medical charts, they stared vacantly through me. I had become a contradiction, a non-entity masquerading as the focal point.

I searched their faces for concern and attentiveness, but I saw only distraction and preoccupation. I saw fatigue in their eyes and exhaustion in what little movement they could muster. As the surgeon continued to speak, I was unable to look away from those weary, disconnected physicians-in-training. The more I watched them, the more troubling and familiar the scene became.

Finally, in those young doctors slouching against the walls of my hospital room, I recognized someone—myself. I had been one of them once, worn down to the point of indifference, wanting nothing more than to leave the room, always hoping the patient would ask no questions. Our time was much too valuable to be spent bantering with patients.

Writing this is difficult for me. I am troubled by the American healthcare system. For most of the years in which I have practiced, the system has been rocked by tremors that are reaching earthquake proportions. Our terminology reflects the seismic change. The art of medicine is now the "delivery" of health care. Family practitioners are "primary care providers," or worse, "gatekeepers." Patients are "customers" or "consumers."

Demand for cheaper services creates demand for greater efficiency, which leads to managed care organizations to oversee how "care" is provided. Doctors merge into large groups or become employees. Hospitals merge with HMOs or these physician groups. All attempt to save money, often at the expense of the patients seeking help.

In the summer of 1995, I became a patient in this system and found it wanting. I have been bewildered and angered by the absence of concern by many healthcare workers for the plight of the people for whom they care. Like other patients with serious illnesses and major surgeries, I sometimes felt reduced more to a disease or a troublesome organ than a human being, a damaged unit to be sent back to the medical assembly line to have a part repaired or replaced.

No doctor asked the questions that needed to be asked: What has this disease done to your life? What has it done to your family? What has it done to your work? What has it done to your spirit? You want people to talk to you as if you are in fact dying, because that is exactly what is happening.

I am a physician. My primary job is to care about the people who come to me, open their lives to me and sometimes give up their lives in the process. I do not realistically expect to find the Jackie Chans of any patient's life entered in a medical record, but I do expect physicians to seek out those Jackie Chans when talking to patients. I expect physicians to connect on a human level with their patients and act not only as doctors but healers, as well.

If we are to be more than skilled, well-paid mechanics, we must ask these questions of our patients. My experience as a patient with a life-threatening disease comes with details unique to my life, but it also comes with universalities common to all people, touchstones that bond us as human beings. I have not seen nor heard nor felt things other patients have not seen and felt and heard before me. I bring only my perspective as a physician who looks at medicine differently now.

I write in the hope that physicians will see their patients somewhere in my experience and ask the needed questions. The answers are profoundly important. I began to discover them in 1994 on an autumn day in the mountains of northern New Mexico.

CHAPTER TWO

Autumn comes early to northern New Mexico's Sangre de Cristo mountains. Winter's forerunner brings a crisp beauty that hints of the alpine cold to come. In September 1994, when we rode our mountain bikes above the Moreno Valley near Angel Fire, summer's green lingered below us on the valley floor, but high on the mountain trail the aspen leaves already had turned to their fall gold.

It was my favorite time of year and I was in one of my favorite places, but I found little pleasure in either. I look back on it with hindsight's clarity and it all makes sense, all of the signs easy to read now that denial and uncertainty have been removed. The alarms had sounded for years, periodically emerging to suggest that I pay attention. I chose instead to ignore them or explain them away. While that behavior certainly was at odds with a physician trained to identify and heed those very alarms, I would learn that it was not at all unusual for a human being trying to decipher the unknown or deflect the inevitable, regardless of any medical training he might have.

I rode with friends that day above Angel Fire, all of us experienced mountain bikers. We began at 9,000 feet, headed for 11,000. We never made it. I couldn't keep up. When I collapsed on the trail, toppling over in a gasping heap, I chided myself for being "out of shape," never connecting the searing pain in my lungs and the weakness in my legs to anything more serious than middle-aged decline.

No one can say when chronic illness begins. More often than not, the earliest signs are subtle ripples in the daily routine of our lives recognized only in retrospect to the more significant disease—AIDS usually begins as a flu-like illness, cancer as a painless lump or generalized tiredness. Physicians look for physical manifestations, aberrations to normal function; they develop predictions and treatment options. Under the best circumstances, though, the period before recognition is difficult to treat and the limitations placed on the physician by a disease's subtle clues are only part of the puzzle.

For patients, this is a time of denial and recrimination as they confront the symptoms and try to explain the body's mysterious changes. When physicians are unable to pinpoint a disease in its earliest stages over an extended period of time, they often will blame the symptoms on psychological factors, leading the patient to believe the problem lies in the imagination—an ailment of the mind, not the body. This reflects the frustrations of the doctor, who, even after performing numerous tests and evaluations, fails to reach a satisfactory diagnosis. The response by the patient is often guilt and anger along with a reluctance to discuss it further. None of this is theoretical to me.

In the earliest stages of my disease, I had difficulty convincing myself or anyone else that something ominous was happening. I associated all of the symptoms with the normal aging process and a demanding lifestyle—a gradual decline, fatigue, stiffness, a decreasing exercise capacity, difficulty in sleeping.

I knew that what happened in Angel Fire was not normal, but I pushed it away and didn't think much of it, even though the first warning signs presented themselves long before the incident on the mountain and continued afterward until catastrophe demolished whatever illusions remained. Those warnings eventually proved their worthiness as subtle prophecies. One in particular came with no small irony.

In May 1995, eight months after mountain biking in Angel Fire, our First Presbyterian Church group in Albuquerque held its annual spring outing at Ghost Ranch, a retreat in northern New Mexico owned by the church. As we were barbecuing our dinner one night, a 13-year-old boy drove frantically into our camp in his father's pickup. His father was slumped next to him in the passenger seat. The boy said his father had suffered severe chest pain while at the Echo Amphitheater, a geologic formation north of Ghost Ranch.

The man almost certainly had suffered a heart attack. While some members of the group tried to calm the boy and assure him that everything would be all right, someone called 911.

There was oxygen and a blood pressure cuff at the camp first aid station, but all we could do was make him comfortable as possible and monitor his vital signs. His blood pressure and pulse were maintaining. Finally, paramedics came and rushed the man off to the nearest hospital emergency room thirty minutes away.

The boy's father survived the heart attack and eventually wound up in the Cardiac Care Unit (CCU) at Presbyterian Hospital in Albuquerque. A month after being discharged from the CCU, he showed up at my office, having learned of my presence at Ghost Ranch. He told my receptionist that he had come in the hope I would take him on as a regular patient in my family practice.

But I was not at work the day he came in. At the very moment he stood at the reception counter in my clinic, I was in the CCU at Presbyterian Hospital, occupying the same bed he had a month before.

It was the summer of 1995. I had begun my formal education as a patient.

CHAPTER THREE

By the spring of 1995 my diminishing physical abilities expanded well beyond my deteriorating athletic skills. No matter the venue—volleyball, bicycling, clinic work, even helping Beth with her gardening—all ended in worsening fatigue.

I had given up most of my sports activities and I was just hoping to get through another day at the office. But at work I was exhausted by midday. I had to sit and rest between seeing patients. The most routine activity became anything but ordinary.

Bizarre symptoms occurred frequently. Painful mouth sores appeared every two weeks, so that I would just recover from one episode only to have another. Eating and talking became difficult. Large red boils broke out on my back, so tender that the slightest touch caused sharp pains. Odd afterimages and flashes of wavy lights periodically obscured my vision; I recall many times while talking to patients that I could not see their faces clearly.

I went to dermatologists and eye specialists. They could not explain my symptoms, leaving me to ask myself the question I had asked so many times before—*What is wrong with me?*

I began doubting myself, wondering whether I had some bizarre infection or mineral deficiency. Or even worse, perhaps my fatigue was "all in my head." At some frustrating point, I began hoping for a disease that would explain everything so I would know I wasn't making it all up. It was not long afterward that I gained new appreciation for an old adage: Be careful of what you wish.

On a Sunday in June 1995, ten months after the Angel Fire episode, we had friends over to the house for a day of tennis and volleyball. I had been active, but I hadn't overexerted myself. We had just finished eating and nightfall was descending, which at Albuquerque's 5,000-foot altitude meant cooling temperatures and relief from the heat of the day. I went into our bedroom to put on a warmer shirt.

Suddenly, two great claws clamped down on my chest, compressing it with such excruciating pain that I could not breathe. I struggled to lie down as the pain exploded inside me. It spread to my neck, into my back and down my arm. I collapsed on the bed and curled into a fetal position. My breathing was rapid and shallow and I wasn't sure if I was panting because of the pain or because I was unable to take slower, deeper breaths. I wanted to call for help but I couldn't speak. I couldn't move. The pain paralyzed me.

A few minutes later, Beth walked in. Wondering why it took so long for me to simply change shirts, she had come looking for me. My back was turned to her, but she could tell I was in great distress. She knew I wouldn't just be lying down to rest. She was shocked at what she saw. She reached out to hold my hands. I was sweating profusely, my skin clammy, my color ashen.

Her voice seemed loud and in it I heard the panic that I certainly felt at the moment. I knew she wanted to get help. Another physician, one of the volleyball players, was still at our house. But I didn't want to make a "scene." I didn't want to attract too much attention. This was a flagrant denial of the reality of what was happening to me, but I told myself that I had no prior objective medical findings to make me worry that something was seriously wrong. I had experienced significant pain before and learned to accept it. When I went for help three years before, the pain had been in my back and shoulders. I underwent medical tests and passed with flying colors; I was told everything was okay with my heart and I came away from the experience feeling like the little boy who cried wolf. Besides, I knew what would probably occur if I did seek medical help. I could just imagine having to go through more testing and doctor visits. Hadn't I been playing volleyball and tennis just a few hours before without any pain or shortness of breath? Surely someone with a serious heart problem couldn't have done this, I told myself.

The pain gradually lessened over the next ten minutes and I continued the process of rationalizing away concern. Beth remained unconvinced. She extracted a promise from me that I would call the cardiologist the next morning as soon as I got to work.

That night I was tired and rundown, a condition by now commonplace, but this time it came with a difference as ominous as it was obvious, neither of which prevented me from ignoring its message. Three years before, the episodes had involved back pain. This one was distinctly in my chest, and so intense I couldn't move to get help—in other words, classic symptoms for heart attack. If one of my patients had described to me the pains I had just experienced, I would have rushed him to the hospital in an ambulance and had him evaluated immediately.

But I was a physician. I thought I knew better. I convinced myself that this episode, while unusually severe, still was only a muscle spasm, so that even with the archetypal signals of heart attack still swirling through my body, I was able to deny reality. I had excellent blood pressure, low cholesterol, no history of heart disease in my family. I had a normal treadmill test three years earlier and had been told by a cardiologist that there was nothing wrong with my heart.

In truth, I was not any different from most men who experience bad chest pains in their mid-years. Even in the face of the most wrenching pains and with many medical risks for heart disease, men often deny their symptoms. "It's only gas, it's only indigestion, I just pulled a muscle," we tell ourselves. (How many men's lives have been saved by determined wives who drove protesting heart attack victims to emergency rooms?)

I had seen this resistance to seek medical attention in my own patients. I always gave them the proper lecture. While working in emergency rooms or the Coronary Care Unit as residents, we young doctors often shook our heads sagely and said, "If only he had paid attention to his symptoms when they first appeared . . ."

It could be said that a doctor should know better, and perhaps therein lies the problem. We know too much and in our knowledge we fear exposing our vulnerabilities, our loss of control, and ultimately our humanness. Rather than being a help in this case, my medical training was a hindrance that allowed me to talk myself out of getting help.

I told Beth I would see Dr. Paul Cochran, a cardiologist, more to appease her than anything. But I was scared, too. Did I really have heart disease? We had met Dr. Cochran at a medical conference and liked him immediately. I began sending most of my heart patients to him and others in his group. At some point I told Beth if I ever needed a cardiologist, Paul Cochran would be my pick. Of course, I said this secure in the knowledge that it would be a long time before I would need a heart specialist. The "long time" turned out to be three days after my terrible chest pain.

I returned to work the following morning, feeling almost "back to normal." As promised, I made my appointment with the cardiologist, but it would be two weeks before he could work me into the schedule, which was fine with me. Now that I was feeling better I didn't think seeing him was all that urgent. Work was hectic, but nothing out of the ordinary. As before, I returned home feeling worn out, which I thought was natural given the pace of the day. I worked for three days. On the third night, the last pretense of normalcy dissolved.

Wednesday was volleyball night. For more than ten years, I had played in the weekly game. I was about to leave the house, but I felt apprehensive about playing. Usually, I looked forward to Wednesday nights and often I was the first to get to the gym. That evening I hesitated, as if my body were telling me not to go. I had worked that day and everything seemed fine, but now something held me back. I paced around the living room trying to persuade myself to go. Beth sensed it, too, and asked what was bothering me. I told her I didn't feel right and asked her to take my blood pressure.

After the first reading, she started over, unsure of what she had seen, though she was more than proficient at reading blood pressures. The numbers were bizarre, wildly out of any range that might be called normal.

She listened to my heart, then handed the stethoscope to me and said, "You listen. I'm hearing a harsh murmur."

Instead of the usual "lub-dub," of a healthy heart, I heard a "whoosh-whoosh." It was so loud I could not hear the normal beats. I held the stethoscope to my chest longer than I needed to, hoping the sound would right itself if I waited long enough. But the sound didn't change. I heard the same loud murmur Beth heard.

I knew it must be coming from a dysfunctional heart valve. The whooshing had to be caused by an abnormal amount of turbulence in the blood being pumped forward by the heart only to collide with blood rushing backward due to the incomplete closure of the valve.

I was not too sure of myself when it came to diagnosing heart disorders based upon sounds, but I could recognize the abnormal well enough to know when to refer to a specialist or have further testing. It was odd listening to my own heart and hearing such discordance. I was Doctor Hsi trying to diagnose Patient Hsi and not doing well on either score.

The next day I called the cardiologist. I tried to explain my symptoms in a clinically detached manner, one physician to another. I downplayed my chest pain. I told him about the blood pressure and how Beth had heard a loud murmur when she listened to my heart.

Dr. Cochran insisted that I come to his office immediately. He was concerned that I was dissecting my aorta, a condition caused by the weakening of the inner lining of the aorta so blood leaving the heart is being squeezed under high pressure into the wall of the aorta itself. If the wall weakens enough, it can rupture and the patient will bleed to death right in his chest.

The cardiologist's office was only two blocks from mine. I remember little of the short drive except the conversation I had with myself in which the subject never changed. *This can't be happening to me.*

CHAPTER FOUR

I lay on my side, watching the display monitor, taking deep breaths when the echocardiogram technician asked. Dr. Cochran had listened to my heart as soon as I arrived. There was no question. It was abnormal. Tests began—EKG, X-ray, echocardiogram.

The black-and-white screen flickered before me for a moment like a 3-D picture that at first glance is a jumble of wavy lines. An image of my heart began to form as the technician moved the transducer on my chest, the heart's walls and chambers easily distinguished by the rhythmic contractions and dilations that were my heartbeats.

Soon I could see the valves separating the heart chambers. I didn't know how to read much from an echocardiogram, but I knew enough to see there was a problem with my aortic valve. I could see the blood shooting forward through the valve and the odd squirt forced backwards through the same valve opening. The technician saw it, too, but said nothing. It wasn't his job to deliver news to the patient, though I hoped for some clue from him and I found his silence foreboding. The task of giving me the bad news would be Dr. Cochran's.

I swayed back and forth from anxious patient to distanced clinician. My mind tried to run through possible causes of valve diseases. I tried to figure out how my constellation of symptoms went along with this finding. I drew blanks.

"You have a mild to moderate aortic regurgitation," Dr. Cochran said.

Confusion and fear made it difficult to accept what I was hearing, but the evidence gave me little choice. So I started horse-trading with myself. I told myself it wasn't really that bad. I searched for a way to minimize the reality's harshness. Perhaps he would do more testing after which he would then prescribe a medication that would control the situation. I clung to the hope that I could resume my life without too much medical intervention. I knew about heart surgery to replace valves. I had patients who had undergone similar procedures, but it had to be fairly severe before this would happen, and my leak was only mild to moderate.

Dr. Cochran said he wanted another test done—a Computed Axial Tomography, a spiral CAT scan. My physician's facade, the protective coating built over years of training and professional standing, slowly gave way to a new identity and new viewpoint. Doctor Hsi surrendered to Patient Hsi, willingly entrusting himself to this other man. I no longer resisted the idea; I came to appreciate Dr. Cochran's soft-spoken thoroughness, relieved to know I was in good hands.

He was so concerned that he personally drove me to the hospital, a courtesy no doubt extended to me as a fellow physician. We made small talk along the short distance, a matter of only a few blocks; we chatted about family and work, neither of us saying a word about the serious business ahead.

We walked into the hospital together, meeting a few doctors in the hallway, but not stopping to talk. I felt disconnected, isolated from a world I was still part of, but one that would never again look the same.

The CAT scan showed no evidence of dissection. Dr. Cochran prescribed two different blood pressure medicines that I was to start that day. He cautioned me about certain activities and told me to lay off too much exertion for a while. He wanted another test, too, a Trans-Esophageal Echocardiogram (TEE).

I was vaguely familiar with the procedure, although I had never witnessed one. A long tube with an ultrasonic device attached at one end is inserted into the esophagus. This allows measurements to be taken through the esophagus from the back of the heart. It is similar to the echocardiogram, but can give better images because the esophagus sits directly behind the heart.

I underwent the test, and having now experienced the procedure as a patient, I think it a good idea for all medical students not only to be professionally familiar with the procedure but to undergo one themselves. It is the kind of hands-on training that will bring them closer to their patients, as well as acquainting the doctors-in-training with their own gag reflexes.

At least now I had a name for my symptoms—aortic regurgitation. If nothing else, identifying it gave me some degree of control. The mystery had been removed. It explained my deterioration, my exercise intolerance and lightheadedness. I felt a strange sense of relief and distress. I finally had a diagnosis to explain my physical problems; but the problems came with myriad complexities. My wish for an easily reversible disease would not be fulfilled.

I was worried about having to give up sports activities, too. The prospect of surgery on my diseased valve was not something I wanted, but taking medications and cutting back my activities indefinitely was frustrating as well. Volleyball, pick-up basketball games, swimming, biking, skiing, in-line skating with Beth and the boys along the banks of the Rio Grande—all of it had been an integral part of my life.

The final test, the TEE, showed nothing that we didn't already know. The valve was leaking moderately and the aorta was dilated, but not enough to warrant surgery. I began the medication therapy. The medications lowered my blood pressure and I couldn't be sure at that point whether my increasing fatigue was related to the medicines or if the disease was worsening. I now had put one toe across the line dividing doctor and patient. I had come face to face with the uncertainty of illness and the turmoil that was changing my life forever. I felt the anxiety that accompanies failing health and I did not like it. Now I was the one sitting on the table in the doctor's exam room waiting to hear the news. All my years of practice had not prepared me for this role—the sick one. My world was turned on its head and all my medical training counted for naught in dealing with my own disease. I was the one fearing the bad news, I was the one praying for a good test result.

In her landmark book *On Death and Dying*, Dr. Elisabeth Kubler-Ross described the stages individuals go through as they approach dying. The first stage, isolation and denial, was where I found myself at that time. I felt estranged from my normal life. I became acutely aware of the differences between me and everyone else. I existed in a world defined by illness. I realized that few of my friends and associates could relate to what I was experiencing. Doctors aren't supposed to get sick and I felt a degree of failure in this. I didn't want to talk about it with anybody.

The medications I took opened yet more windows into the patient's world. I was given three different blood pressure medications, medicines I had prescribed to patients in the past and medicines Beth had studied in her pharmaceutical research program.

They made me sick.

The numbers in the patient information inserts that came from drug manufacturers to reflect the risks of side effects— 1 percent, 2 percent, 3 percent—printed in microscopic type in packets we had opened hundreds of times before, suddenly became more meaningful. Until now abstractions in barely readable typefaces, the minuscule chance of a negative reaction to medication became everyday reality for me. I couldn't tolerate the medicines and I swore to never again take lightly a patient's complaint about side effects.

Kubler-Ross' second stage of dying is anger, but I postponed this step and instead went directly to the third stage—bargaining. I kept thinking that if I would slow down and if I would try to be a better person, my illness would abate. I prayed that God would have mercy and spare me the agony of watching my health wane. If my illness would resolve, I'd dedicate my life to service and good works. I'd go to church more often. I was ready to deal.

Bargaining did make me examine my life more carefully, but this faint hope proved to be even less than wishful thinking. Instead of improvement, disaster awaited.

On Monday, June 19, 1995, I awoke before sunrise. I was panting, my breaths shallow and rapid. I sat up and my breathing slowed. Still groggy from sleep, I lay back down only to find that once again I was having trouble getting enough air. I sat up again and felt better. Finally, I found that by propping my head up on a couple of pillows I could lie back down.

I was too sleepy to comprehend what was happening to me— heart failure.

When I awoke about an hour later, I felt better and went to work. I managed to finish my workday without incident. That night I fell asleep easily.

In the early morning, I awoke again with a start. I was definitely short of breath. I could feel my heart pumping madly in my chest. I was suffocating and the only way I could get enough air was to sit up and lean forward. There was no denying it now. I was experiencing a classic symptom of heart failure known as paroxysmal nocturnal dyspnea and orthopnea, the lungs' inability to get oxygen into the bloodstream and the heart's inability to deliver it to the tissues of the body from a flat position.

Within hours of waking up, I was back at the cardiologist's office. Dr. Cochran was out of town. Dr. Robert Dubroff was on call. He listened to my heart, then repeated the chest X-ray and transthoracic echocardiogram. I will never forget his terse words.

"You are in heart failure," he said.

The valve problem had worsened significantly in only three weeks. He said he would call the CCU. I was going to the Presbyterian Hospital cardiac unit immediately.

For the first time, I began to panic.

"We're going to have to replace your valve," he said.

As well-practiced as I had been in the art of denial, it was no longer an option for me. This was serious and it was happening to me. I was going to the hospital. I was a patient with congestive heart failure.

CHAPTER FIVE

I watch myself walk into the Cardiac Care Unit at Albuquerque's Presbyterian Hospital. I wear the same clothes in which I work every day, the casual, relaxed style Dr. Hsi wears to see his patients. I am the healthiest looking person in the CCU. Some of the nurses and doctors in the unit recognize me and call out greetings. I am in a comfortable environment, one in which I have been at ease for many years. But at noon on that summer day in 1995, I have not come to visit a patient. I *am* the patient, and the cold reality of it leaves me in a daze.

A nurse gave me a gown. As I went through the motions of undressing and surrendering myself to the system of which I had been a part for so much of my life, I thought it incredible that I was only hours away from having my chest opened up. I couldn't grasp it, I couldn't process any part of such an implausible notion.

Nurses came into my room. Some I recognized, some not. All treated me gingerly and with courtesy. The ones who knew me undoubtedly considered me (and Beth) to be "one of them," and I suspect they passed the word to the others who didn't know me. No one said as much, but I had the feeling they looked at me and saw themselves. One of their own had fallen. As a result, they treated Beth and me the way each of them would have wanted to be treated, which, of course, is the way any patient should be treated.

They got my IVs going, they drew blood, they pasted electrodes on my chest, hooked me up to an EKG monitor, gave me medications—and suddenly, my status as a patient had been formalized. I sat there in an official, open-backed gown with my butt hanging out for everyone to see. Someone handed me a urinal. Measuring output was a routine procedure for heart failure patients. I did exactly as I was told. I followed every instruction, debated no one, second-guessed no one. I wanted to be a good patient.

The surgeon came to see me. I had never met him before.

"I'm really sorry you're here," he said.

We spoke about the surgery scheduled for the next morning. It would take four to five hours. He gave me three heart valve options: porcine, human cadaver or mechanical. Each had advantages and disadvantages.

With any type of animal or human tissue, I wouldn't have to worry about anti-coagulation because there was little concern about blood clots forming. Infection was less of a threat, too. These valves are also the closest to a human's own natural valve. The downside was that in ten years I'd probably be looking at a replacement, and being young (I was forty then) I'd probably need it done again. Biological valves are not as durable as mechanical valves and they usually take longer to insert than the mechanical valves, which means the patient is on bypass longer and increases the surgical risk.

A mechanical valve was potentially lifelong. They rarely broke down. The biggest disadvantage was that I'd be on Coumadin, a blood thinner. Because these mechanical valves are not natural to the body, they may cause clots to form that can travel from the heart to other parts of the body causing pulmonary emboli, arterial occlusion or strokes. To prevent this, patients must take anticoagulants (blood thinners) every day for the rest of their lives. Blood clots are a leading cause of serious complications in post-surgery patients.

Patients on chronic anticoagulant therapy must have frequent blood tests to finely tune their clotting times, which must be kept within a fairly narrow range. When taking Coumadin, just about anything can change the body's response to the medication; eating certain foods, taking other medications (almost any other medication), fever, alcohol, or a change of environment. Another drawback was that it could affect some of the activities I'd want to pursue. Patients taking blood thinners are supposed to avoid situations or activities in which they could be injured for an obvious and chilling reason: death by bleeding.

I did not want to come back to have this done again. I chose the mechanical valve.

About 2:30 in the afternoon, Beth went home to check on our sons, Andy and David. While she was gone, I ended up drawing the kind of attention no patient ever wants. I was trying to raise the bed up and the cord got caught in the IV controller, twisting around the apparatus until it brought the whole unit crashing to the floor. There was an awful electrical smell and nurses came rushing in and quickly moved me out to another room. No one said anything about the clumsy physician-patient they had on their hands. I was thankful.

Beth stayed with me that night in the hospital room. We passed the time watching television, but if someone had asked me the next morning what we watched, I couldn't have remembered. The nurses brought in one of the recliner chairs used in the recovery and rehabilitation rooms. The chairs fold out and can be made into a bed. Beth pushed the recliner-bed up against mine, but the match was less than perfect. They weren't the same height and the side bars on my hospital bed were raised. We tried to hold hands through the bars. Finally, Beth just crawled into my bed and we talked into the night about when we met and when the boys were born. We cried a lot, too.

I wondered what would happen to my sons if I didn't live through the next day. I wanted them to be happy. I wanted them to be educated. I wanted them to know the things that are worth knowing, much of which they would learn from no university but only from our family life. I wanted them to love God and for Him to have a strong presence in their lives. I wanted them to listen to their hearts in their relationships with others and to apply their many talents to the benefit of others less fortunate than they. I wanted them to be passionate in the pursuit of their dreams and to stand up for what is right, even if no one else does. I wanted them to think for themselves. More than anything, I wanted them to know how much I loved them and how proud of them I was and how much joy they had brought to my life.

I didn't sleep much at all that night before surgery. Sleeping is difficult anywhere in a hospital. The environment doesn't encourage it. First, there's the underlying anxiety about the surgery itself. Then there's the constant hustle and bustle of the nurses, especially in a Cardiac Care Unit where they must check patients continually to get vital signs. When you're taking a lot of medications, as I was at that point, they have to wake you up in the middle of the night to give them to you.

In some respects, I was still Dr. Hsi even then. Presbyterian was the hospital in which I practiced. Outwardly, my identity remained as a doctor. But in the solitude of my mind, lying in a hospital bed on what might be the last night of my life, I knew otherwise.

The nurses seemed a little intimidated because of my physician status, though I had done nothing to provide any evidence of intimidation, except for breaking their IVs. It is not my nature to intimidate anyway; and I did not want to be offensive to them or make them uncomfortable. The nurses and other medical staff are good at what they do. I had to trust them. I had no desire to boss them or direct my own care. So I hung back and tried to treat them with respect.

I was scheduled for surgery early the next morning, but typical of less urgent heart cases, I kept being pushed back. It was past noon when the surgery finally began. The delay turned out to be a harbinger of things to come and would be repeated in the next two heart surgeries as well.

The tension is brutal. Family and friends wait, apprehensive and tongue-tied. Conversation is next to impossible. No one knows what to say. So they sit and wait, just as the patient sits and waits, like ballplayers pumped up for a game only to be told it's been delayed because of rain.

You've made up your mind that this is going to be, that this *has* to be. Then you spend interminable hours wondering if it will ever be.

An orderly came to get me around ten-thirty. Someone asked me to remove my wedding ring, glasses and watch. I gave them to Beth. She put the wedding ring on a chain and slipped it around her neck, where it would remain for the next week because when I returned from surgery, my hands were too swollen to wear it. It was a difficult moment for us, as it must be for any patient and a loved one. In the final minutes before taking the patient to surgery, these last intimate items that are so much a part of his identity are stripped away and replaced with an odd-looking surgical cap and a mound of warm blankets.

The orderly wheeled me out into the hallway. Beth and my mother followed. We were packed into the elevator with other staff and visitors. No elevator is reserved for transporting surgery patients, so at that critical moment when there are so many things you would like to say, you can't because strangers are crammed around you and your loved one.

For reasons I still do not understand, the lingering image in my mind is that of the ceiling tiles passing by as the orderly wheeled me down the hallway. Each time I think back to that surgery, I see ceiling tiles passing by smoothly above me; I hear the voices of unseen people coming and going as we make our way along the corridor.

When we got on the elevator with the crowd of doctors and other patients, I tried to look around to see who was there. I recognized faces and when they saw mine, they clearly were surprised, though I don't think they had any idea why I was there.

The orderly pushed me into the holding room, a long, rectangular space, cold and antiseptic, where patients who are next on the schedule are taken just before being brought into the operating room. If any anesthesia procedures need to be completed prior to surgery, they are performed here. My mother said good-bye as we went in. Beth was allowed to accompany me, an exception to policy we gladly took without asking any questions. Beth stayed for about forty minutes, the only time we had that might be described as belonging to us. From the moment we woke up that morning in the CCU, the room swarmed with people. There were no moments to touch or whisper to each other.

Several of the operating room staff introduced themselves and explained what their role in the surgery would be. The anesthesiologist made no assumptions about what Beth and I knew because we came from medical backgrounds. He explained everything he was going to do before he did it. He remarked on how tough my veins were, an observation I would hear repeated frequently in the future. He left, but returned soon after with paraphernalia for inserting yet another line. He placed the arterial line in my right radial artery (wrist). Arterial lines are used to directly monitor blood pressure and to obtain blood samples. Inserting this line is an involved procedure and he had a great deal of difficulty. It took two attempts before he got it in.

Surgery began at 12:40 P.M.

The circulating nurse in the OR called out to the waiting room by telephone every hour or so to talk to a family member. The first call told my family I was under anesthesia and the incision of the sternum and pericardium had been completed. The surgeons had cut through the middle of my chest wall from about the notch at the upper edge of the sternum all the way down to a few centimeters below the bottom of the sternum.

The second call came after I had been placed on bypass and my core temperature lowered to 32 degrees C (normal body temperature is 37 C). My heart had been stopped and the valve replacement procedure had begun.

Beth knew it would be more than an hour before the next call and she stepped out to get something to drink. She could not know that just about then the surgeons who examined my heart discovered this would be no simple valve replacement.

The echocardiograms and CAT scans done three weeks before indicated that my aorta was about three centimeters, but it was in fact more like six centimeters, a dangerous degree of distention; and unlike many aneurysms, mine was thick-walled, while most are thin-walled. The surgical team now knew it was dealing with some other process in the aorta itself.

The lead surgeon (and friend) Dr. Chris Wehr left the operating room to find Beth. When he finally tracked her down in one of the hospital's labyrinthine hallways, her medical experience once again became a double-edged sword. She knew as soon as she saw him in the hallway, still in his surgical scrubs, that something had not gone according to plan. She should not be bumping into the lead surgeon in a hallway.

He needed to talk to her about complications that had arisen, but the hallway was noisy and busy, full of hospital staff and visitors waiting for elevators. He took her arm and guided her into a nearby stairwell and closed the door. He told her that in addition to the valve I would need to have my ascending aorta replaced. The ascending aorta was fibrotic, severely inflamed, with extensive, irreversible cell damage and distended much more than they had anticipated. At that point, he did not know if there was any involvement of the aortic arch. He said they had never encountered anything like this before.

The surgical team called in Dr. Richard Garrety, the senior and founding member of the group. The plan was to replace my damaged valve with a device made by the St. Jude Medical company, which at the time was the most widely implanted valve type. A composite graft made of tubular synthetic material would be attached to the artificial valve. The valve end would be sewn into the aortic root after the coronary arteries had been temporarily detached. The coronary arteries would then be sutured back into place (this is called "replanting the corns"). The other end would be sewn into the aortic arch (or wherever they could find viable tissue) after removing the diseased ascending aorta.

Dr. Wehr told Beth that this was a much more difficult and extensive surgery than what had been originally planned. The risks would be greater. He needed her verbal consent to do these added procedures. But the request was only a formality. What choice did she have? I was in there with my chest open and an aorta that was falling apart in their hands.

Almost five hours later the surgery ended and I was wheeled into the recovery room, where another profound experience awaited me.

—∿—

It would be a long time before I felt comfortable enough to talk about what happened next—the bright light. Even now, I broach the subject with trepidation, knowing that while I am certainly not the first to report such a phenomenon, the experience invariably is met with skepticism in some quarters, especially by my colleagues in the medical community. Nonetheless, I can only report it as I remember it.

It wasn't as if I were separate from the light but more a part of it, a peaceful, quiet place. I had a strong sense of consciousness, yet I don't recall any sense of physical body within it. I was in a place flooded by a pure, radiant white light, brighter than any light

I had ever seen before. Time had no meaning. I felt warm, secure and at peace. I sensed the presence of other *spirits.* (Unscientific and as mystical as it may be, I cannot think of a more appropriate word.) They communicated with me somehow, but not with voices. I didn't hear them speak, but rather felt the contact. Somehow they were familiar to me, yet I cannot name anyone specifically or define the meaning or method of the communication. I can say only that I felt an astonishing, abundant love.

I would experience this bright light again after another procedure and I would come to see the experience as a clear message from God. My faith would become unshakable and it would no longer matter to me what people thought when I spoke of it. With time, whatever fear I had in speaking of these things disappeared when I found that upon hearing the story, people usually were eager to hear more.

When the light ended, it ended quickly. In an instant, warm comfort gave way to harsh coldness. Tubes sprouted from my chest, a catheter invaded my bladder, and all around me, foreign sounds I could neither identify nor locate assaulted me. I had a tube in my throat and the ventilator breathed for me. If I tried to breathe on my own, it would override me and take over, dictating its own pace, which often created a sense of panic.

I slipped in and out of consciousness, but never went back to the light again. I woke up for good around two in the morning.

My chest incision was closed and the skin held together with surgical staples. Beneath the skin, thin wire held the edges of the sternum together. In most bypass operations, the procedure can be done through the aorta itself, but in my case, because they would be operating on the aorta, they had to go through the femoral artery in my groin. An incision was made there to put in the big arterial IV lines.

Near the end of the procedure, the surgeons poked holes through my chest wall after repairing the valve and aorta. As they prepared to close, they pushed two clear plastic chest tubes up around my lungs. The tubes prevent fluid from accumulating in the chest. About a centimeter and a half in diameter and several feet long, they came out from the bottom of my rib cage on either side of my chest and were connected to bottles in which blood and other fluid drained.

Two thin pacemaker wires resembling common telephone wire came out of my chest at the bottom of the breastbone. The wires were placed on the surface of my heart and brought out through my skin so they could be attached to a pacemaker if my heart started beating erratically.

I had been told about all of this before surgery and, indeed, had seen it happen to numerous patients. I was well aware that tubes and wires would be coming out of my chest when I woke up, but the consequences had not registered. To some degree, I had a medical curiosity about all of it when I awoke and saw these alien objects sprouting from inside me, but there also was the fearful realization of how my body had been so insulted—the huge incision, the holes where the tubes came out, two pacemaker wires growing from my chest, IV lines, a big special line that went in a major vein in my neck through which medications were administered and to monitor pressures in and around the heart, the arterial line in my wrist measuring blood pressure, a tube through my nose that ran into my stomach to prevent bloating or vomiting, and the final insult, a tube in my bladder to drain away urine—all very typical in these surgeries, all looking very different when it's your body from which they grow.

When Beth was allowed in to see me about an hour after I was wheeled into recovery, it was as if someone had punched her. She reached out to a gurney to steady herself. When people come out of any surgery, but especially open heart surgery, they have been practically frozen during the procedure and when they arrive in the recovery room, they are gray and ashen, almost waxen, like a body in a casket. They look dead.

Beth found it hard to look at me, even though in her long nursing career she had not only seen hundreds of patients in exactly the same condition but had assisted in the insertion of the same kinds of tubes and wires that now protruded from my body. Critical necessities when she was a nurse, they had been transformed into barriers keeping her from a loved one. Wanting only to hold me, she remembered a child who had drowned in a swimming pool cover. The baby had been put into a protective metal "cage" in the Intensive Care Unit before he died. Tubes and wires protruded from his tiny body. The infant's mother had pleaded to hold him and the memory of it now came rushing back to Beth. Wanting only to hold me, Beth had to content herself with touching my hand, the only contact the barriers would allow.

What have we done to you? she thought.

Nurses work hard to empathize with their patients. Until Beth saw me in the recovery room, she thought they could. She doesn't anymore. She believes they are compassionate and do wonderful work with patients, but they cannot know what the loved one does. They cannot know the aching emptiness of wanting only to hold someone in their arms. No one had prepared her for this.

As for me, "helpless" is the word that comes to mind.

Physically, you are restrained, a medical prisoner. When you have a tube in your throat, you can't talk, you can't communicate. You feel as if you have no control over anything. I don't believe doctors talk to patients about this. The profession does not acknowledge how utterly helpless patients become and how much at the mercy of their caretakers they are. I simply was not prepared to be that helpless.

The lights were dim in the room and a nurse had been talking to me, but I can't remember anything she said. My chest hurt and I couldn't move in any way that would be comfortable except to lie flat on my back. Even if I had been given the freedom to move, I didn't have the strength to turn myself.

The catheter in my bladder kept up a continual burning and caused a sensation of always having to urinate. It felt as if there were ground glass coating the tube. After awhile, the tube was disconnected from the ventilator, but remained in my throat in spite of my breathing unaided at the time. It wasn't until the tube was taken from my throat that I began to entertain such lofty ideas as "comfort."

It was probably mid-morning the next day before I was fully cognizant of my surroundings. At Presbyterian they have what is known as the Intensive Recovery Area. The patients are in one large room in which you can see everybody. They're separated only by curtains for privacy. Beth came in with my sister-in-law. Then my mother and later my brother came. It was fairly uneventful except for the catheter in my bladder and a seemingly unquenchable thirst, a phenomenon of anesthesia. The nurse wouldn't allow me to drink because of possible regurgitation or even worse, aspiration into my lungs. I kept asking for ice chips and adjustments on the catheter. I was consumed by those two things: thirst and the burning sensation of the catheter. They were so uncomfortable and so compellingly important to me. Eventually, those symptoms went away, but I don't remember how long it took.

I was moved to semi-private room on the floor around 1 P.M. My roommate suffered from emphysema and had a loud, rattling cough. Conversation was difficult because the other patient and all of his visitors could hear every word that was said. My throat was sore from the ventilator tube and I couldn't talk much above a whisper. While the economics of semi-private rooms are understandable, I was relieved when I was moved to a private room three hours later. The room was an amenity reserved for hospital staff if there were no patients in need of it. I would spend the next five days there reflecting on the radical turn my life had taken.

I didn't know before surgery what my disease was. Going in I thought I had a relatively simple valve problem. At some point in the recovery area, somebody told me I had a disease—Takayasu's aortitis. The final diagnosis hinged on the results of the pathology report in combination with the clinical findings. It took over a month before we knew for sure that it was Takayasu's.

Aortitis is a general classification that refers to an inflammation of the aorta, the largest of the arteries. Several different diseases may cause aortitis, one of which is Takayasu's. But at the time of diagnosis, I had no idea what it was and I am not sure that anybody else knew much about it.

Takayasu's is a rare inflammatory disease that has a predilection for aortic tissue. It is thought to be an autoimmune disease, although the exact cause is not known. The inflammation of the arteries eventually can cause blockage of any or all the vessels of the aortic arch.

Generally, the first symptoms are global: fever, malaise, loss of appetite, muscle aches, weight loss. As the disease progresses and the inflammatory process begins to involve the large arteries, the initial signs are replaced by symptoms related to the arteries involved. For example, if the carotid arteries are affected, the patient may have visual disturbances, dizziness, and a brief loss of consciousness because the circulation to the brain is compromised. If the arteries beneath the clavicle are affected, then the patient will probably experience numbness, intermittent muscle aching, and loss of upper extremity pulses, which happened to me when I had no right radial pulse.

Destruction of the aortic tissue can lead to aortic aneurysm, as it did in my case. The disease is aggressive and death from congestive heart failure, stroke, or aneurysm rupture often occurs within five years of diagnosis. Takayasu's usually is seen in young females under the age of 40. The median onset age is 25 years. The incidence is 2.6 cases per million patients per year.

In other words, I had a rare disease, and rarer still for a 40-year-old male.

Those days after surgery were a period of reflection for me. I was unsure what direction my life was going to take. I thought a lot about my wife and my kids. I started having doubts about whether I could return to work, and what it would be like if I didn't, and what I would be like as a father to the boys. When all of this weighed so heavily on me, two nurses took the time to sit and talk to me. (One later became a patient of mine.) Our conversations were not of life and death but of kids and families. It was a wonderful connection.

Of course, I spoke often to Beth of these things. I told her I wasn't sure where my life was going. I didn't know what this illness was and I didn't know its implications. People reassured me that everything looked positive, but no one really knew much about it, though our education was proceeding rapidly.

At some point, the pathologist invited Beth and me to look at the slides from my heart tests. The tissue samples were taken from the aortic valve and the aorta during surgery. Beth said that even her untrained eyes recognized that the cells were grossly inflamed and deformed. But the diagnosis was still not firm at this point. There were a number of other possibilities, but Takayasu's was the clear front-runner.

My cousin, Dr. David Hsi, a Harvard-trained cardiologist, called every night and tried to find out as much as he could about the disease. He worked hard doing things I would not have thought about. He arranged to have my tissue slides sent to Beth-Israel Hospital where a world renowned pathologist could look at them to provide another opinion. He talked to cardiologists caring for me in Albuquerque and let them know he wanted to be involved. To the Albuquerque cardiologists' credit, they were very good about doing this. I have known doctors who find this sort of outside interest in their cases personally offensive or somehow an affront to their competence, but the doctors caring for me were understanding about it.

Before going home, I would be introduced to one more indignity, one more piece of evidence that too often the human being we know as the "patient" is looked upon as something inanimate to be fixed, a machine with a part gone haywire.

A nurse cut the sutures holding the tubes and wires in place in my chest. A physician's assistant from the cardio-vascular surgery group then walked in, introduced himself perfunctorily, abruptly informed me that he was there to take the tubes out and didn't say another word except to tell me to take a deep breath.

Then he put one hand on my chest for leverage and with the other hand yanked the chest tubes out. He repeated the act again with the pacemaker wires.

He did it quickly, but it was painful. It felt as if something inside of me had been ripped out, which is exactly what was happening. It lasted only a few seconds, but to say it was traumatic is an exercise in understatement.

I never saw him again. I remember the moment being impersonal and cold. He was efficient. He did his work and left. But I don't think it is better that way. When you are going to inflict that degree of pain on someone, you should at least make an effort to let the patient know you have some concern about what's going on.

This experience was classic and there would be more to come, each mirroring the other in at least one critical respect— the patient as machine, something less than the sum of his broken-down parts.

On July 4, five days after the surgery, I went home.

CHAPTER SIX

While I could make no claim to independence, I looked forward to freedom nonetheless. Presbyterian Hospital had treated me well, but the interruptions that are a staple of the hospital patient's life made it impossible to be comfortable. I was eager to leave. I longed to be in a familiar place. I wanted to go home. When I got there, I found lessons on assumptions waiting.

The first two days revolved around pain radiating from the chest wound itself. My sternum was weak and I could feel movement where normally there would have been none. The only position that might be called comfortable was flat on my back. Moving hurt too much. I couldn't lie on my side. I couldn't use my arms because any kind of pushing movement brought nauseating waves of pain radiating from my chest wound. I was weak. I always had assumed that post-operative patients could at least read a book or watch TV to pass the time while recuperating. I was wrong. I could not focus on anything, not even to watch television. A restlessness lingered for months after the surgery. I couldn't read, I couldn't sit still. It was easier to just lie there.

A few simple pleasures took on added luster—my first shower, replacing the sponge baths that had been the routine; the ability to get up and urinate on my own instead of being forced to use a urinal or a catheter. It stung a little bit, but felt good.

Ultimately, these simple pleasures, or more to the point, their absence, came down to questions of autonomy and control. Physically, they brought comfort, psychologically even more. It felt good to know I could take care of my own bodily functions. I felt as if I had won myself back, liberated myself from the illness that had consigned me to the control of so many others. But this newfound freedom came with an unsettling sense of something not yet finished.

An incompleteness remained. We knew it was Takayasu's, but what came after the diagnosis? Was it simply a matter of taking this out and taking that out and putting this in and suddenly your disease is over? Or was there more to it?

I didn't have that information. I didn't know what to expect post-operatively. Few doctors in Albuquerque had experience with Takayasu's. Most of them tried to reassure me that once they had taken out the diseased portion that the body would have nothing left to attack. But my doctors made assumptions, too. They didn't really know what we were dealing with.

So the question remained: What next? I wanted to believe it was all over, yet something seemed unresolved. I was certain of it.

Still, I was home, looking forward to the familiar, and none more so than the Fourth of July fireworks display the kids put on each year in the street in front of our house. I had come home on one of our favorite holidays and I was excited about it. Beth made a quick trip to the grocery store and the local fireworks stand where she bought the biggest box of fireworks she could find. The kids picked some of the greens and vegetables that grew in abundance in our garden. When Beth got home, she threw burgers on the grill and we picnicked in the backyard with my brother and his family.

But the day ended early for me. My energy faded in the afternoon, sapped by the heat and excitement. By sunset, I was exhausted and in bed. A late afternoon shower had cooled the air and a soft breeze carried the scent of sage through the bedroom windows. I could hear the grown-ups and their children gathering outside on the street.

Kid laughter erupted as the first sparklers were lit, followed by the sounds of dancing feet on the pavement as the kids traced neon pictures in the dark. Then came the whiz of pinwheels and cracking of poppers punctuated by the hiss and whine of bursting rockets. I could hear the *oohs* of the children as the fireworks were lit and the clapping of hands when the glittering light of a favorite floated to the ground.

I got up once to look out and breathed in the faint smell of the fireworks. A low flat cloud of luminous smoke hung above our street. I was sad not to be there with them, but delighted to hear their laughter. I had been isolated and removed physically from them during my hospitalization and I had forgotten how they served as a lifeline for me. I had forgotten how their laughter reflected something we adults socialize out of children—joy.

I always had been out there with them in the past. I was the one who lit the fireworks and helped clean up and nagged the kids about being careful and warned them not to get too close and to wait until the flames of the Roman candles had burned down before running out to set up the next ones. I had done all the things parents do with kids. It was hard to be close enough to hear the sounds of that joy but not be a part of it.

I remembered a time when it seemed as though summers like this one would last a lifetime. A sense of melancholy pervaded me as I stood at the window. I felt I had lost something in my life, a certain vitality, maybe even a loss of hope for the future. It wasn't something I could identify and engage, but more an unfocused fear that I wouldn't be able to enjoy the future as I once thought I would.

Two days later, that sort of introspection led to a conversation with my brother that we never had before.

Andy sat in the living room and watched the Wimbledon tennis tournament on TV. The kids played outside and we had the house to ourselves. I had called him to come over to check me because I was getting nervous. I had begun to get chilled easily. I took my temperature and I was running a fever of about 101. Sometimes a low grade fever like this is expected after surgery, but the prospect of infection is not to be taken lightly, especially after heart surgery.

My wounds were swelling and draining a little bit. The one in my groin was particularly puffy. The wound in my upper chest was swollen and red; a pinkish fluid seeped out from both the top and bottom of the incision, which I assumed was nothing to worry about, given that I'd never been through this before.

Andy listened to my heart and looked at my wounds, checking for signs of infection or pneumonia. He found neither, and my fever had come down to near normal.

After he finished examining me, he stayed for a while and we chatted. Somehow the talk turned to our childhood in Clovis, New Mexico, a small town on the eastern border near Texas (so close in geography and culture that New Mexicans refer to it as "Little Texas"). We had never talked about these things before and I still don't know what brought on the conversation.

He said my illness was significant to him. We are close in age (he is 20 months older than I am) and though he never said as much, I believe I brought him face to face with his own mortality. We talked about our parents and what it was like for us growing up. Our conversation rambled from one subject to another spontaneously.

In some ways it was calming for me. But Beth had overheard much of what we said and it frightened her. She said it sounded like I was reviewing my life, as one might do when he is preparing to die. Perhaps I was. My foundation had been rocked, the base upon which my existence was built shuddered, as if a seismic event had loosened the fittings that held my life together. I was apprehensive and could not rid myself of my unease. Something wasn't right and I had no idea how to fix it. Beth said my words sounded almost like a confession I was using to reconnect to my brother and my past.

That evening changed my relationship with Andy. It brought a cleansing and closeness I had not known before. We broke through all the old competitions and rivalries we had collected over the years.

By the end of the night, I came to see that I not only could survive these things, but I could learn from them and put them to use when dealing with my patients. Once again, I found that my patients and I were not so different. Our conversation eventually changed the way I practiced medicine. For the first time in my life I had let my guard down. I had talked openly of vulnerability and weakness and fear.

As a rule, I don't believe people do what Andy and I did. People generally don't talk about the difficult things, the doubts and worries that linger in our hearts, particularly about people we've grown up with. As the night wore on, Andy and I visited those places. I think we were getting to know each other in a way that allowed us to express our love and caring for each other. By going through all those shared experiences and finally sitting down and talking about what it all meant to each of us, we touched one another.

It was a precious moment for each of us and only one of many changes in my outlook forced upon me by the radical turn my life had taken. I had conversations with friends and family that never would have happened had I not become so sick. At the top of the list are prayer and spirituality. Had it not been for my illness, I never would have examined these questions the way I did.

This time marked the beginning of an openness in me, a time when I was willing and eager to discuss spiritual questions.

I began first to reflect on myself, then inquired among friends, and finally, when I went back to work, I found myself ready to bring up these issues with patients when the circumstances seemed appropriate.

I realize this may not come as a revelation in the course of human history. Confronting one's own mortality routinely causes people to reassess their lives and what truly matters. Routine or not, the importance of those questions—prayer, spirituality, family—isn't diminished by the conditions that brought them to the forefront.

The morning after Andy examined me, I called the cardiologist to discuss my symptoms. He said they could be a common postoperative problem and that it wasn't unusual for someone with this kind of surgery to have some partial collapse of the lungs, adding that the collapse in and of itself can cause a low grade fever, a somewhat routine finding for a few days after surgery. If the symptoms persist after four to six days, then it's something to worry about. He said that if it happened again, he wanted me to call immediately and that in all likelihood I would have to go back in the hospital.

That night the fever returned. Tylenol helped bring my temperature down. The normal rhythms of the body typically cause people to have fevers in the afternoon and evening rather than in the morning.

The next morning, I called Dr. Diane Sansonetti, though for the simplest of reasons I did not want to: I was scared to death of what she might say. My symptoms could have been caused by infection, which would mean more surgery. I could be headed back to the hospital. Dr. Sansonetti was in the cardiac surgery group and on call that day. She was not directly involved with my case, but she was familiar with it. I described my symptoms to her. She gave me the answer I anticipated and dreaded.

"I'm sorry," she said. "You're going back to the hospital immediately."

They had to confirm that I didn't have infection on the new valve. If they couldn't, in all likelihood we were looking at redoing my surgery. The implications of this were bad—another valve, more antibiotics, and a good possibility I would not survive. There is up to a 46 percent mortality rate in a new post-operative valve replacement patient with the kind of infection I now feared.

I needed to leave without delay. What would we do with the boys? We didn't know when we would be coming back. We needed to close up the house. We thought of dozens of things that should be taken care of, but there wasn't time. A call to a friend solved that problem. She came over. She told us that a member of our fellowship group from the First Presbyterian Church had attended a prayer circle for a friend with a serious illness. She asked me if I would like our group to arrange one for me. I said I would have to think about it. We exchanged hurried hugs and I climbed into the car.

On the way to the hospital, Beth and I talked about the prayer circle and quickly dismissed it. Neither one of us had attended one, but in our view such things were a final resort, a last ditch plea for a dying person. We felt they smacked of fundamentalism. Beth had visions of tent revivals and fire and brimstone preachers. We had faith in modern medicine. That was what would "fix" me, not good friends praying. Beth called her later and told her that we didn't need the prayer circle.

It was Saturday morning, four days after the Fourth of July. Beth drove, and a good thing, too. On the way to the hospital an embarrassing insult was added to the already serious injury. The big sack of fluid that had developed in my groin popped open and soaked my pants. It's called a seroma, a collection of fluid in the wound. A post-operative complication that is not generally serious by itself, it provides an excellent culture medium for bacteria. It also makes an embarrassing mess out of your pants and adds yet one more small humiliation to a list that needs no more.

At the hospital, I was hustled into a wheelchair and I wound up in the same room on the cardiac floor that I had the first time, which was fine with me. It had become almost familiar territory and if I had to be back in the hospital, I was glad to be in the same room.

A nurse who had taken care of me only the week before started an IV immediately and drew blood cultures to monitor for infection. It was touching in a way. She knew the potential for catastrophe that my readmission represented and she seemed so sad to see me back. When I was wheeled into the room, the doctors and nurses already waited for us—the infectious disease doctor on call, a cardiologist, a cardiac surgeon. Everything had been pre-assembled in anticipation of my admission.

I had never met this particular cardiac surgeon. Before he was through, it would have suited me just fine if I never saw him again. As the other doctors stood by and watched, he took a syringe with a needle and jabbed it down into my groin and pulled back on the plunger to see if he could get any fluid out. He got very little. He jabbed the needle into the lower part of my chest incision with the same result. He removed the surgical staples from the upper portion of my chest wound, picked up a scalpel and cut open the wound. He gave me no anesthesia.

Beth said it would have been easier to watch them torturing me. I turned white as the sheet under me and I sweated profusely. When he opened the upper part of my chest wound, it felt like he had picked up a knife and carved me open right there, which in truth is what he was doing. But even now, I am tempted to lapse into the well-trained physician's euphemism—*discomfort*—to describe the effect of his opening the chest wound and probing my groin with the needle. Not only do I find the euphemism far too tame, but I am somewhat amazed that given my experience I would consider using it at all. At the very least, the consideration is testament to the physician's training that teaches him to be distant and dispassionate in all matters, even his own agony.

The wound had been troublesome before this, but it did not bother me that much as long as the edges were together. When he reopened it, all the nerve endings came alive. It was excruciatingly painful and to this day I don't know why it was done with no anesthesia. An IV already had been started. It would have been a simple matter to give the medication through the IV line.

Even more puzzling, neither Beth nor I said a word in protest, not so much as a single question, a situation that would repeat itself over and over again throughout my surgeries and hospitalizations. Like so many patients and family members before us, we remained mute in the presence of the physician.

But then so too did the other doctors and nurses in the room. Obviously uncomfortable, and some more than a little pale at the scene unfolding in front of them, they looked down at the tops of their shoes, leaned against the wall, shuffled their feet. No one said a word.

My whole (inexplicable) attitude was "I'm just going to tough this out," which had sort of been my outlook all along. I didn't want to complain and make a fuss. These people were my colleagues, and they stood by silently, waiting to see what he found, which turned out to be nothing conclusive.

More tests were ordered. They found nothing alarming.

An echocardiogram meant to search for signs of vegetation on the valve or apparent damage at the graft site indicating infection showed nothing of the kind. Another chest X-ray came back negative, as did the blood and wound cultures. Still, the doctors expressed concern. They started me on three antibiotics to ensure that if this were an infection, the antibiotics would take care of it.

Sunday passed quietly in the hospital and we breathed a little easier. Beth and I thought I would be discharged the next day, another exercise in wishful thinking.

That Monday Dr. Robert Dubroff, one of my cardiologists, came in with several other doctors. I hadn't had any more fevers and I was feeling pretty good.

This is great, I thought. *This is going to be a relatively minor hospitalization. They'll check me out and send me home.*

After the other doctors left the room, Dr. Dubroff slipped back in and said he wanted to set up for another Trans-Esophageal Echocardiogram (TEE) later that afternoon. I asked him why, though the expression on his face clearly suggested his reasons would be troubling. I told him his partner had said the regular echocardiogram was okay.

He said the regular echocardiogram was *not* okay. They thought they saw a small area that was cause for concern because it might represent infection.

Beth came in shortly after that and I told her what Dr. Dubroff had said. It frightened her, too. She knew the consequences of infection as well as I did.

The TEE wasn't scheduled for another four or five hours. Beth called my family and a few other members of our church fellowship group to let them know. Our emergency babysitter, who was a member of the fellowship group said she would call the other members.

By eleven o'clock, I was tired and wanted to nap before lunch. Beth, restless and searching for something on which to expend her energy, said she would pick up Thai food for lunch. Asian food was comfort food to me and she knew it. On the way back, with her arms full of Thai take-out, she ended up on a elevator with one of the heart surgeons who had operated on me. He was about the same age as I and had kids the same ages. I always had the feeling he was sympathetic to what I was going through. My situation seemed to hit him in a big way, though neither of us ever discussed it.

He told Beth, "I want to be very honest with you. If we have to go back in and operate again, there's a 50-50 chance he won't survive."

When Beth returned to my hospital room with all that wonderful Thai food, neither of us felt like eating.

The church fellowship group asked again if I would like the group to hold the prayer circle. At that point, I was scared and ready to do anything that might improve my chances. I told them to go ahead and arrange it.

They had never done anything like it before, but they felt it was a good way to help. It had been about two years since we joined the group, a dozen couples from our church who have children of similar ages. They called themselves Thank God It's Fellowship. When we first joined TGIF, it functioned on more of a social level, but that changed over the course of my illness. Once a month we gathered for a potluck at the home of one of the members of the group or for some other activity. We roller skated together, went camping and hiking. Beth and I formed close friendships with several of the couples and spent time outside the group with them as well. All of them soon would become critically important to us.

It was a Monday when Beth called them and many of these people were at their workplaces. Yet each said, "I'll be there." People dropped everything they were doing and came to the hospital. They met in the chapel that afternoon as I underwent the test to determine if there would be a second heart surgery.

The prayer circle was loosely defined. It was simply a matter of people forming a circle and members praying in any way they wish. Beth always had been uncomfortable with the idea of public prayer, as many people are. Beth and I attend church regularly and our family routinely participates in church activities, but Beth's medical and scientific background mediated against public displays of religiosity. She had never considered herself a "religious person," whatever that elastic phrase might mean. Nonetheless, she attended the prayer circle that day, and found it one of the most profound experiences of her life.

A close friend and member of the fellowship group, someone we looked to as a spiritual leader, led the prayer circle. It was only later that she confessed she'd never led one before in her life. It was a subdued affair, which went a long way in alleviating Beth's uneasiness. About twenty-five people attended, sitting quietly, until the prayer circle leader began speaking. From that point, anyone could speak to the group or simply offer a prayer. The gathering lasted about forty minutes, convening about the same time the hospital staff was upstairs setting up for and performing the TEE that would be the deciding factor in whether I would go back to surgery.

She began by praying that the doctors would find no signs of infection and that I would not have to go back to surgery and would be able to go home to recover. She asked the group to visualize my heart and ask for healing. At some point she said something to the effect that it was okay to be mad at God and that opened the floodgates for Beth's anger. She ranted at God, accused Him of being unfair, asked how He could do something like this to me. Soon everyone spoke. Beth and I were filled with gratitude for each of these compassionate friends who dropped everything they were doing to be there for us. They generously shared some of their most intimate feelings and profound beliefs in that small hospital chapel room. We felt blessed. It was the first of many such life-affirming experiences.

Beth left the chapel with a sense of strength and the belief that somehow they'd been heard. She called my hospital room from the lobby to see if the procedure had been completed. To her surprise, I answered the phone, recovered enough from the anesthetic to give her the good news myself. The TEE results were negative; there was no infection. I could hear the cheers through the phone.

A great burden had been lifted. Beth came back to the room in tears. She said the prayer group had been touching and meaningful to her. She had never experienced anything like it. Neither had I. It gave me hope. It made me feel wonderful to know that so many people cared so much.

It was during this time that the group decided "We are going to help this family out."

They took in our kids, fixed our dinners, mowed the lawn, ran errands, defrosted our refrigerator, answered the phone, changed a flat tire, washed our clothes, fixed a leak on the roof, and pruned trees. They gave me an appreciation for friendship I never had before. One loaded his lawn tractor into a horse trailer once a week and drove to my house to cut the grass. Other TGIF members joined him, trimming bushes and trees and pulling weeds. They worked until dark. It went on like this all summer.

They told Beth to worry only about taking care of me; they told me to worry only about getting well. It took a tremendous load off my mind, in spite of the irony that at times I could hardly stand to watch them working in my back yard.

Perhaps it is only human nature (or only the nature of the human male), but even in the face of everything I had been through and the obvious truth that I was in a physically weakened state, a part of me still didn't want to admit I couldn't handle these things alone. It is a mystery I have not yet solved and the incongruity of it was my constant companion. No matter how compassionate and generous these people were, it would never be easy for me to watch them do what I felt I should be doing.

Being around people in crisis is difficult. It puts us uncomfortably close to our own mortality. It can be awkward and unpleasant. Most people try to avoid situations where they might be too close to something like this, but these good friends didn't. They picked up the slack whenever they saw the opportunity. They gave up time at work. They came on holidays, weekends and in the middle of the night to care for us. A community came together and said, "We will be here for you."

And so I set about the business of healing.

The chest wound the surgeon had opened would stay open because once opened the way mine had been, it must stay that way to heal by "second intention." (The open wound granulates in and is gradually covered by new skin cells forming a scar.) My muscles could be seen underneath the wound and it initially required dressing changes three times a day in order to keep it moist and clean.

I was going to have to wait until it closed by itself, which would be a matter of many weeks.

I went home again with an overwhelming sense of gratitude. Not only had I been told there was no infection, but now I had seen something I had never seen before—community, the power of prayer and spirituality. It was greater than anything I had ever known or expected.

CHAPTER SEVEN

"We have to do something to calm this disease down," Dr. Eddie Benge said.

With the threat of an immediate second surgery removed, I had gone to visit Dr. Benge, an Albuquerque rheumatologist. Because Takayasu's is a kind of autoimmune disease, he was the specialist I needed to consult. He had treated two young women afflicted with Takayasu's and he had been in consultation with a doctor at the Cleveland Clinic who was familiar with the disease.

Dr. Benge's choice of therapy—prednisone—came as no surprise to me. I was familiar with the drug and had prescribed it to my own patients on numerous occasions. When he said I would be taking prednisone, it did not occur to me that the medication would breed a threat to my marriage and family.

Prednisone is used to combat many types of inflammation, such as arthritis, skin disorders, and asthma. It is a powerful medication with potent side effects and it would become yet another hard lesson for me to learn, another example of how the practitioners of my art sometimes do not or cannot appreciate the ramifications of their best intentions.

He put me on 60 milligrams per day, a high dosage. Normally, physicians prescribe prednisone for the short term, ten days or so and then the usage ends. Typically, the patient will start at a high level, taper down and then stop. In cases of chronic or more significant inflammatory involvement, patients will go on high doses of prednisone for months or years.

At the very least, I would be taking the drug for several months and possibly even after a year.

The point of the drug was to suppress my body's defensive attack on the aorta. The problem was that it also might suppress my own immune system and weaken my body's ability to heal itself, a dilemma that created its own peculiar conflict. If a patient has a wound, as I did from the heart surgery, and prednisone is prescribed to control inflammation, the therapy pretty much guarantees that it will take a long time for that wound to heal. The open wound that spread across my chest was six inches wide and ran the length of my sternum. It was, in fact, a large crater, exposing muscle and fat tissue.

I knew these things about prednisone, but until then the knowledge I had was that of a physician. I mistakenly thought I understood its side effects. But I did not understand them at all. I knew only what I had studied, what I had read, what I had heard from patients. "Side effect" was about to become a phrase I never would look upon quite the same way again.

Insomnia came first. I tossed and turned all night, repeatedly getting up at two and three in the morning and just sitting in the dark. I tried to read, but I couldn't concentrate long enough to read anything. I would pick up a favorite book, read a paragraph, find my attention wandering and put the book back down.

My skin felt oily and greasy. I couldn't keep myself clean, or at least feeling clean.

Then I started gaining weight.

One of the classic changes prednisone brings about is the development of a "moon face," a condition in which the patient develops fat deposits in the face and cheeks. Then the patient starts losing fat and probably muscle tone in the arms and legs.

All these things happened to me.

I felt weak and soon began developing acne, another common side effect. My appetite changed. I was hungry all the time. "Ravenous" might be a better word. Before going on the prednisone therapy, I never snacked between meals. Now it was huge bowls of ice cream before going to bed every night. I ate a bowl of cereal an hour before dinner. I ate potato chips and candy, big bowls of buttered popcorn. I ate enormous portions at meals. I grazed through the kitchen from the time I got up until it was time to go to bed.

After my doctors started reducing the prednisone dose, my eating tapered off, but initially it was alarming. I had always insisted on healthy food prior to this. It wasn't just the amount of food I was consuming that was troublesome, but the types of foods as well.

Dr. Benge had warned me that the side effects would begin immediately, especially in terms of sleep. I tried to take him at his word. He had expertise with this and I knew nothing about the disease, though I was familiar with the trade-off we make in medicine: Are the benefits of the drug worth the side effects?

My cousin, Dr. Kareen Lowder, an ophthalmologist at the Cleveland Clinic, said prednisone seemed to be the recommended therapy. The clinic had been conducting Takayasu's research and Kareen had access to the results because of her interest in the ophthalmologic changes that occur with the disease.

So I was in no position to argue about prednisone. I was just going to have to go with it. Nonetheless, the side effects presented daunting challenges, and before long, other side effects appeared that would dwarf any physical complaint I might have.

Prednisone causes psychological problems. Some people go into a kind of psychosis; some develop a significant euphoria, a kind of hypo-manic condition. I became obsessed with keeping the house clean and not having anything lying around. If anyone came into my house now, it would be clear that this is not how we live. We are the parents of two active boys and the kids always have things out, as boys everywhere do. Before I began taking prednisone, this never bothered me. Now it made me mad.

I was volatile and I was taking much of it out on the kids. If David, who was then seven years old, left out a single Lego block, I went ballistic. I never became violent, I never struck them, but the boys had to make tremendous adjustments that year. They found themselves in the company of a stranger who looked frighteningly like their father. They had to tiptoe around me. Their home, once comfortable and safe, had become an emotional minefield.

It was no less so for Beth.

Our marriage had never been like this. We each had a temper and we'd had our disagreements, but what was happening to us now was so alien to anything in our past as to look like a work of nightmarish fiction. I flew into a rage over the smallest thing. No one, least of all me, could predict when it would happen.

A fight in the kitchen comes to mind. I don't even remember what it was about. I was angry about something left out in the living room, I think. Beth was cooking dinner. Before the shouting ended, she was crouched in the corner of the kitchen floor, her arms crossed around herself, crying hysterically. It made me even angrier.

The kids had fled to some other part of the house. It makes me sick to think about how they felt—frightened—hearing our angry voices, hiding in their rooms. The more Beth begged me to stop, the madder I became, screaming, standing over her, slamming the flat of my palm against the cabinet doors. Then, suddenly it ended. Beth continued to cry. I left the kitchen and found a room to myself.

No one ate dinner that night. Each of us spent the evening sequestered in our own private hell. Later that night, when Beth came into the bedroom, I lay on the bed. It was my turn to cry now. She put her arms around me and we clung to each other. I told her I had scared myself. I didn't know what was happening to me. I felt helpless. Exhausted, we both finally fell asleep.

That night's scene was repeated a number of times over the next six to nine months. We never talked to anyone about it until we finally went into counseling.

A day or two after the kitchen fight, Beth asked me to talk to Dr. Benge about the side effects of prednisone. It was becoming clear to her that what we were living through was more than just the stress of critical illness. When I did eventually ask Dr. Benge about the emotional side effects of prednisone, I remember him being surprised at the question. I think he expected me to be aware of it already. He described instances with other patients where the prednisone made them do things out of character. He talked about extreme personality changes found in some patients taking the drug.

In hindsight, we should have sought counseling much sooner than we did. We were struggling to get by on a day to day basis. We had no perspective. Because we were in the middle of it, we didn't make the connection between the prednisone and my behavior until later.

If only someone had asked . . .

Time and again I return to that thought and reflect on the trauma that would have been avoided. Hence, this story. Maybe someone who reads it will think to ask the next patient.

I stayed on prednisone for seven months at high dose therapy; it would be almost a year before I tapered off into an alternate days program, which is preferred with patients requiring chronic therapy. The plan usually is to give daily, high dose therapy until the desired effect is achieved. In my case, that meant until signs of the Takayasu's abated. Then I was to switch over to alternate days. I was kept on a constant steroid dose on one day while gradually reducing the level of prednisone on the alternate days. This was kept up until the alternate day dose was eliminated entirely. It was a slow process with a complex dosing plan and the powerful medications had profound effects on my body. The quality of my daily life was totally dependent on what was happening with my prednisone therapy.

The tapering off was mandatory. The patient cannot simply stop taking it. Take prednisone over a long period of time (longer than the standard 10-day therapy) and it shuts down the body's production of steroids. Stop the drug cold turkey and you become extremely sick.

The drug eventually became a joke among our friends, who learned to inquire whether the day would be a prednisone or non-prednisone day for me. On a prednisone day, I usually had more energy; on a non-prednisone day I did fine until about noon, when the medicine would begin to wear off and I would feel run down. As my energy drained, I became irritable, achy, and sometimes had minor fevers. Soon I would be cold and stiff and not be able to do a thing about it but wait for the next round of prednisone. Often I would just go to bed at six o'clock in the evening and hope to sleep until the next morning when I could take my next dose.

On one non-prednisone day, Beth and I made the mistake of arranging a dinner date with friends. We went to one of Albuquerque's finer restaurants. The evening ended prematurely in one of those good news-bad news jokes: The good news was that I didn't fly into a rage at a waiter; the bad news was that I fell asleep in the middle of dinner.

The dependency on the drug quickly became too much like addiction for me, but there was nothing I could do to stop it, and it was not the only debilitating medication that had become part of my daily life. When I came home from the hospital, I was on three antibiotics intravenously through the special catheter. It took four to five hours a day to administer the antibiotics. I would start at five in the morning so I could spend some time with my family before the kids went off to school and Beth went to work. When the house was empty except for me and our three cats, I would to try read but couldn't. I would try to sleep and remain wide awake. The antibiotics went on for six weeks. I was also taking Coumadin, a blood thinner, and for a little while, Vasotec, a medicine meant to keep my blood pressure low.

I was bothered terribly by New Mexico's summer heat. I was being told to get out every day for a walk. I made a habit of going out at seven or eight in the morning because if I waited until around ten o'clock, the heat wiped me out. I could not tolerate it. It exhausted me and my heart rate sped up. In the back yard, our swimming pool beckoned to me, but I had an open wound and couldn't slip into the cool water.

I wasn't depressed, but I was discouraged. I wanted to be out doing things with the kids and Beth, but all I could do was sit in the house. I had become so preoccupied with everything going on in my life that I no longer had the ability or capacity to think about other things, and I had lots of time to think. Sometimes, I felt an overwhelming sense of suffocating anxiety and helplessness. I was afraid that if I gave in to it I would lose hope. I often felt isolated, stranded. I seemed to alternate between a desperate need for company and days when all I wanted was to be alone.

To say it was a tough time for my family is to engage in flagrant understatement. The truth of the matter is this: I was in a position to lose my family.

When I came home, I had a dressing over an open chest wound that Beth needed to change two and three times a day. Some of the IV antibiotics I was taking were toxic and had to be run into the body slowly through small piggy-back bags of IV fluid with the medication in them. All of this required complicated preparation.

With each dose, the set up and running time took from 45 minutes to an hour, four times a day. The dosing times were set up so I could deliver two of the medications back to back. This way I could have two-hour blocks of time where I was free of the IV pump, a cumbersome device that limited my mobility.

If I wanted to do anything else while receiving the medications, I had to drag the IV pole and its heavy pump everywhere I went. So I developed a routine. I gathered everything I thought I would need for that dose and settled into a comfortable chair in the guest bedroom. We moved a small refrigerator and my medications and other supplies in this room and it became my treatment room.

The first six weeks after coming home I spent most of my time there. It had a big window that looked out into the rose garden in the backyard. I had always loved that garden. We had planted about thirty rose bushes in it and they bloomed profusely that summer. Beth, an avid gardener, planted a yellow rose bush in a spot where I could see it easily. The roses' soft beauty, so much a contrast to the harshness of the medications coursing through me, brought a comfort difficult to describe. But their soothing beauty was short-lived.

Because the IV medications were not compatible, we had to be careful that we didn't mix them in the tubing. This required yet another ritual. We had to flush the IV line with a neutral solution, clear the antibiotic line, hook up and administer one antibiotic, flush again and use the same sterile technique each time.

Anyone who has a "central line," as I did, is at risk for infection. The line goes directly to the body's central circulation, as opposed to a peripheral IV that might be in an arm or hand. The central line catheter is threaded into the vein close to the heart. If a bug gets into the system, a life-threatening septicemia could develop very quickly.

It was critical that Beth adhere to a strict sterile technique with all of these procedures because my immune system was suppressed by the prednisone therapy and I had to be especially careful to avoid infection because of my heart valve.

I had three dressings: one over the open chest wound, another over the groin incision, and one over the central line insertion site. Each dressing required a different technique and different setup.

Beth dressed the open wound with a "wet to dry" dressing. (Wet gauze is placed next to the skin so that the gauze doesn't stick to the wound and pull off the top layer of newly granulated cells when it is removed. A dry gauze is placed on top of that.) She used a dry dressing on the groin incision. The central line dressing required antibiotic ointment and a dressing material similar to Saran Wrap with an adhesive backing. With its sterile drapes, gloves, syringes, instruments, dressings and ointments, the routine demanded precision and skill.

These daily rituals exacted a terrible emotional price.

Almost universally, patients who suffer from critical illness regress emotionally. Dump prednisone into the mix, stir it up with a physically and emotionally spent spouse, and you have a lethal combination. It almost destroyed us. It was the worst period in our marriage.

The damage done to us lasted far beyond the actual period in which Beth was responsible for my physical care. She felt trapped in a situation over which she had no control, a condition I believe is common among caregivers. Throughout the six weeks that I required intensive care at home, there was a battle of wills between us.

Each of us experienced anger and resentment for our own reasons. The bitterness between us was tangible. Often, while performing these procedures, which required so much physical contact, we would not exchange a single word. We filled the silence with cold anger. When she put that last piece of tape on, she would escape the room emotionally exhausted. At other times, she became perfunctory, creating a self-preserving distance, another common pattern I believe family caregivers experience when tension levels rise.

One memory in particular comes to me with painful clarity. It begins on a long treatment day, a day on which all the dressings and the IV lines required changing. It took about an hour to complete all of the procedures and we'd had a few snappish words about the dressing change earlier in the day. We wouldn't find what lay at the heart of those words until months later in counseling.

But on that Saturday, there was only anger, a simmering bitterness that fed off the tension created by serious disease and its consequences. Home had always been our sanctuary. My disease transformed it into our crucible.

Beth spent the morning doing chores that had been piling up all week. She wanted the afternoon to work in the garden, which was not only her refuge but played a large role in transforming our home into a thing of tranquil beauty.

Normally, we saved the long treatment day procedures for late in the afternoon but I wanted Beth to change the dressings earlier than usual so I could do something that seemed terribly important at the time. I can't remember now what it was. Probably watch a TV program, as I was unable to do much else.

When I told her I wanted to move the dressing time up a few hours, she reacted predictably. We were so much on the defensive with each other that a certain tone or a narrowing of the eyes was enough to set the other off. We tiptoed around each other. We made talking about these things a self-fulfilling prophecy. By expecting a certain reaction we ensured we got it. In this instance, I expected her to get angry, she did, and off we went. She glared at me. We exchanged words.

She wanted to work in the rose garden. She hadn't worked in it for weeks. I asked her what was more important, her roses or my health.

"What do you think?" she said.

She turned on her heel and went back outside.

I watched her through the window. She walked to the garden, her spine stiff with anger, and she began working. When the time came for the dressing change, she didn't come back inside, but stayed in the garden. I was furious. Ten minutes passed, then twenty.

I went to the back door. I watched her stab her trowel into the dirt. I *told* her to come in. It was not a request. It was a command. She looked at me for a long moment. I stared back. I wasn't going to let her "win" this one. I was right and she was wrong. I felt that if I lost this battle, I could lose control of our relationship. That I was even thinking in these terms, "lose control of our relationship," was evidence enough that a severe distortion had come into our lives. At the time it was all happening, I remember feeling a need for control. Up until then my relationship with Beth was balanced. We made decisions together. Certainly there were times when we struggled for "power," as all couples do sooner or later, but overall, we made our way together, sharing that power, exercising give and take until we arrived at a mutually acceptable decision, regardless of who might be perceived as the one "making" the decision.

All of that changed when I got sick. I needed to be the one dictating the terms. Everything in my life had spun out of control. I was facing death and with it came a compulsion to exert control in every area I could, a common phenomenon in many people with chronic illness. We saw it often in dialysis patients. Even in the smallest, seemingly irrelevant details, patients became exacting and picky. You had to place that glass of water on the night stand in exactly the right place or the patient might have you move it four times before the patient let you go.

Beth dropped the trowel and walked past me into the house. She didn't speak. Neither did I. I followed her into the bedroom. I laid down on the bed and she began changing the dressings. Our cold, mutual silence continued. I stared at her throughout the procedure, willing her to look at me. She avoided eye contact until she was in the middle of changing my chest wound dressing. I moved my head and she looked up. Our eyes locked and I knew she could see nothing but smoldering anger in me.

She stared back at me, defiant, her resentment as strong as mine. Without taking her eyes from mine, she stripped off her rubber gloves, flung them to the floor and stalked out of the bedroom without looking back. She left me there lying on the bed with my chest wound still open. She didn't return. I changed the dressing myself.

We didn't speak of this until six months later in counseling. When we did, neither one of us could talk about it without crying. To the outside world, we looked fine. No one asked, no one knew, no one had any idea what had become of our lives. What we did to one another in those wretched times is beyond description. I thank God we survived it, but I will never understand how. I look back on it with incomprehension. I love Beth, she loves me, and I will never understand how or why we abused one another the way we did. I know only that in the crushing pressure brought to bear on families in situations like ours, dangers exist that all physicians should be aware of and be willing to ask about. These questions are crucial. Patients' lives may depend on them.

Until we sought counseling, we could not or would not talk about what was happening, which only intensified the sense of isolation we both experienced. Later, in speaking with other people who have been patients or caregivers, we learned that this cycle is not uncommon. If only we had been able to acknowledge our feelings, it would have been a first step to resolving some of the guilt and anger.

The disruption to the family was profound. The boys got little or no attention from us. We were concentrating on just making it through one minute at a time and the kids were lost in the shuffle. They began to fight more and the escalating conflict between them added to the family strain. In essence, they had been abandoned, too. This was where our friends really stepped in, some of whom included the boys as a part of their families. In hindsight, it was probably better for the kids not to be in an atmosphere fraught with so much tension.

It remains remarkable to me that no healthcare provider ever asked how we were coping with the burden imposed by the complicated care I required. There is a tremendous need for psychosocial intervention in cases like ours, but it is rarely offered. (I suspect there was an assumption that because Beth was a nurse, she could handle the stress of the complex medical procedures needed daily).

Dramatic changes in the healthcare industry and increasing numbers of patients with disease and disability have imposed demands on family members who must assume responsibility for the care of their loved ones. Family caregivers have become an important part of the healthcare delivery system. They are the ones now who must provide care that in the past had been given by health professionals. With managed care a dominant force in the healthcare industry, it is highly likely that the numbers of family caregivers will increase. In these times of shortened hospital stays, families are often left to fend for themselves. It is critical that we recognize the problems unique to these families and develop mechanisms for supportive clinical intervention.

When we were trying to make arrangements for home care shortly before I left the hospital, friends took Beth aside and told her she had stretched herself to the limit. In addition to caring for me, she had the boys to watch over, her work with a clinical trials program she was establishing and the management of my practice. She knew that families often were encouraged to bring in visiting nurses (our insurance covered the expense) to help with these complicated medical procedures. A family member certainly can learn the techniques, and even may be an expert in them as Beth was, but there are still deep emotional factors tied up in all of it.

Two close friends suggested Beth discuss this with me. When I got home from the hospital, she did. I responded with nothing less than emotional blackmail. Anything remotely related to my care had become potentially explosive. I ricocheted from anger to ambivalence. I told her that part of me wanted her in the house to take care of me and another part of me knew she had to take care of our family and ensure our financial well-being and to take care of all the other things in her life that needed attention. I didn't want to hear her concerns. I wanted her to take care of me, and if she didn't do it then she didn't love me. I thought she was selfish. Didn't she know how helpless I was? Didn't she know how much I needed her reassurance that she was there for me no matter what?

She felt as though I had no appreciation for the strain she was under and that she was proving her love for me every day and that I didn't care. She felt her needs no longer had value or meaning. It was not the care itself that bothered her, it was a matter of being heard, of recognizing that she, too, had valid points to be made. She said later that if I had been willing only to talk about the pros and cons of bringing in a home health-care worker to give her some relief, she would have willingly provided the care I now demanded. I wouldn't discuss it. It wasn't an option in my mind. Beth had to do it and that was that. But we knew none of this at the time. We knew only that the battle lines had been drawn.

None of this behavior is defensible. All of it is a tangle of fear, medicines, pain and uncertainty.

She agreed to continue administering the medications and providing nursing care by herself, but later said she resented the way in which I had pressured her. I continued with my already well-documented behavior—almost daily explosions fueled by drugs and anger that ensured the emotional minefield in our house was still a dangerous place to walk.

By the time September rolled around, I had begun to regain my strength and there was a respite for everyone. But the underlying tensions did not go away. They had never been addressed. Our relationship had become fragile and we were afraid to talk about what was really going in. On the surface we celebrated my recovery while our souls withered.

To our friends, we looked like a couple who had overcome a catastrophe. We had challenged the illness and beat it. Everyone around us thought we were doing so well. No one knew about the bitterness that threatened to suffocate us.

Why couldn't we talk about it? Why didn't we reach out to someone? The reasons are complex. In part, we thought other people had been through similar crises and survived and we should be able to survive, too. We were healthcare professionals. I was a doctor. Of all people, we should have been able to do this.

I believe if only one person in the huge array of healthcare providers we were surrounded by had taken the time to ask, "How is this affecting you?", the floodgates would have opened. But few doctors know how to draw such thoughts and feelings from patients, and fewer still have an interest in doing so. It would have been such a relief to talk to someone about it for both of us.

Around the middle of the month, my wound finally closed. It had been two-and-a-half months since the day the surgeon pulled it apart until six inches separated its two sides. My walking program progressed from a mile to five miles. I had begun to run, too, though my doctors and insurance agent would not have approved. But I was determined that I would not bow to the disease. I had been athletic all my life and I was not going down without a fight. So I ran.

We started eating healthy food; we ate meals at the same time every day, always taking care to avoid the long list of foods that could interact with my Coumadin and affect the time it would take for my blood to coagulate. I took vitamins. I stuck to a rigid schedule with my numerous medications, never missing a dose. I kept my frequent appointments with doctors. I followed all of their instructions to the letter. I went to bed early every night. I started meditating in an effort to counteract stress. Our household revolved around these routines.

I went back to work two days a week in November. I tried to be positive, but I wasn't sure the disease was whipped. I continued to have symptoms, most of them flu-like: achiness, fevers, fatigue. Some days they were severe enough to keep me in bed. Most days they were milder.

The constant was their persistence. They were with me almost all the time and the days I felt well were rare. I don't know exactly when it happened, but at some point I became aware that I had forgotten what it was like to feel good. I had become accustomed to feeling lousy and it always was hard to know why. Our dilemma was trying to distinguish where the symptoms came from. Was it the disease? Was it the prednisone? Was it the absence of prednisone? Had I just caught a virus? Every symptom was magnified, its significance blown out of proportion because of its possible implication. Nothing could be taken for granted. I was worn down and struggling to get the proper perspective.

At home, just under the surface of everything else that pummeled us, an unimaginable nightmare hurtled toward me.

The burden of my physical care had been lifted, but I was still on the high dose of prednisone. The unresolved anger and resentment still festered. Beth made an appointment to see our pastor, Rev. Paul Debenport. He told her we needed counseling immediately. When she told me she had spoken to him, I reacted predictably and lamentably. I was angry that she had aired our "dirty laundry" publicly, though a confidential meeting with our pastor hardly amounted to anything public.

As we continued to speak about her meeting with him, it took a few minutes before a word she used made its way through the cloud of anger that enveloped me—*suicide.*

Beth said she had taken no concrete steps toward it, had made no preparations for it, had not seriously considered it—but she thought about it every day, the suggestion of it randomly floating into her mind at some point in the course of her day. It staggered me to realize that the pressures brought to bear on our household had created an atmosphere in which something so grotesque might surface. The wounds created during those first few months had not healed. We had established an uneasy peace that enabled us to get by day to day, but we were trying to heal a deeply wounded relationship with a Band-Aid. We began seeing a counselor immediately.

CHAPTER EIGHT

"Puzzling" became a cornerstone of my medical liturgy. I heard the word used first by a cardiologist on call the morning after my eyes inexplicably crossed.

We were on the way to a Chinese New Year dinner. I was driving. Suddenly my eyes crossed and I found myself sitting on the shoulder of an Albuquerque freeway, sweating profusely, nauseated, unable to see or think clearly, my hands clenched around the steering wheel, 18-wheelers rocking the car as they roared by. Beth and the kids were as frightened as I was.

My eyes righted themselves within five minutes and my vision started to clear, but I was left scared, weak and shaken. The next morning I was back in the cardiology clinic.

"Puzzling," the cardiologist said.

No explanation could be found. Two months later my eyes crossed a second time, again when I was driving.

Another round of tests began.

I saw a neuroophthalmologist, who did a thorough exam. I had an MRI and an MRA. I had ultrasounds on my entire body.

Every test indicated I was fine. There was nothing abnormal.

The neuroophthalmologist could not explain the double vision.

The cardiologist said everything looked good.

The rheumatologist said everything looked good.

Finally, because somebody had to say something in the way of a diagnosis (an unwritten medical law), I was told it was "stress."

In other words, it was all in my head, a too-common practice among my colleagues, I fear. If doctors can't find anything definitive, they say (some in kinder ways than others)—*It's all in your head.*

Regardless of origins, the succession of odd, unpredictable episodes continued. I had sharp but short-lived pains in my back. I suffered brief losses of short-term memory. I was driving David to school and suddenly I could not remember what medication I was taking. I found myself having to concentrate fully on the task at hand. I had to consciously remind myself that I was taking my son to school. I had to think hard about which streets to turn on. I was following the same route I had driven for years. I recognized little.

It was not the first time something similar happened. That the episodes were brief and minor did nothing to lessen their impact. I would blank out on common, everyday things that should have been well known to me—our address, a familiar phone number, the name of a friend. I had been a person who could remember a patient's lab values from the previous year. If I looked up the telephone number for a pharmacy at seven in the morning, I could recall it twelve hours later. If my son, Andy, and I worked on a homework math problem, I'd remember the numbers for a week.

When I could not remember how to drive David to school, I was well aware of what was happening. But the more I grappled with it, the more anxious I became. I couldn't think clearly and felt disconnected from the world around me. By the time I dropped him off and got to my office, my mind had cleared, but the incident left a residue of uneasiness. It is strange indeed to have memory simply disappear.

I went to a neurologist. He could not explain what had happened and I found myself in familiar territory again—self-doubt. The same questions arose that challenged me before I was diagnosed with Takayasu's.

Is there really something wrong with me? Or am I imagining it all?

I had no desire to see another doctor. I didn't want any of them to tell me everything was okay and come away from the conversation feeling as if I'd jumped the gun. Unable to explain what was happening to me, the doctors gave me reassurances instead and I went along with the charade. What else could I do? I had been given every test in the medical book and every test said I was fine. It wasn't so much a matter of doubting the physicians as accepting that they were unable to find out what was happening and it was now time for me to get on with my life.

But that choice creates doubt and guilt. If I can't figure out what's going on and they can't figure out what's going on, difficult questions begin.

Am I not living right?

Am I not eating right?

Am I exercising too little?

Am I exercising too much?

Am I not getting enough sleep?

Am I working too hard?

All of these things come and with them comes uncertainty.

Could I be imagining this? If I am, how do I correlate imaginary symptoms with double vision?

I sometimes have patients come in and tell me they're tired or they have aches and pains or they are having memory problems. I tell them I understand and order tests. I might suggest the patient has been under an awful lot of stress (there's that word again) and I will ask if that element could be playing a role in the problem. After the tests show nothing, I will say I can't find an explanation for it and for now we have to wait until something definitive arises.

I now understand how my words must have sounded to those patients. I was getting the feeling that my doctors were beginning to doubt me, too. I would undergo the tests and nothing would show up and at times I wondered if the unspoken response from physicians was "You're making this up."

I thought back to January, seven months after my surgery, when my cardiologist said doctors who don't understand something tend to blame the patient for the symptoms. He said he found it common for physicians to simply think the patient was wrong.

We don't have a problem, they tell the patient. *You have a problem. We've done all the tests. We can't find anything wrong.*
I was now like so many frustrated patients who had traveled this path before me, trudging from doctor to doctor, getting more and more frustrated.

Some of the symptoms I was willing to accept. They could be explained by my lifestyle. They could be explained because I was under stress. But double vision? How did they explain that? I had never heard of people with psychosomatic illness complaining about double vision.

The answer to this lies in doctors getting to know patients better. To be fair, it must be said that doctors have been burned believing patients who magnified their illnesses or complained of illnesses that didn't exist. Physicians have gone to great lengths to discover what is there only to find there was nothing there to begin with.

Consequently, doctors tend to go to that end first, saying the illness is imagined or exaggerated when they can't explain it, rather than going in the opposite direction and saying *we* can't explain it. Our best approach now is not to keep ordering more and more tests, but to tell patients we believe them. Sometimes that's enough.

I believe. It is a simple thing to say to a patient.

You have a problem and right now we are unable to tell you what it is.

I would feel better if I were a patient and I came out thinking they believed me.

I have no hard feelings about any of the doctors I saw in the course of my treatment. They were kind and treated me well, yet somewhere along the line there was this sense that they thought I was making it greater than it was, that I was magnifying it. I am certain of this.

In the months'-long upheaval that followed my first heart surgery, I probably learned more about being a healer than in any other time in my medical career. We need to talk to our patients about much more than the diseased valve or the ailing kidney. But to suggest such involvement on the physician's part runs counter to our nature and our habits, learned long ago in medical school. Physicians are trained to deal with the tangible. We like to work with body parts. When we get into emotional things, we feel we are out of our depth and we simply don't want the patient to know that we are out of our depth. We like to maintain the upper hand. When physicians have a personal conversation with someone about issues such as those that racked our family during much of 1996, they are forced to break down the barrier they have worked so hard to construct and maintain.

The simple truth of the matter is that we cannot separate the patient from his environment. The patient's world and his illness are woven together. How we respond to the threads that make up a patient's life affects recovery. We need to ask about family; we need to include loved ones in discussions about care. When we walk into an examining room or a hospital room, we need to be aware that in all likelihood, the patient will not be asking questions, no matter how diligent we may think we have been in encouraging it. So we must anticipate the questions.

Patients do not come to us in a vacuum. If we are to be more than physicians, if we are to be true healers, we cannot treat them as if they do.

What this means to me is not only taking all the wonderful resources and knowledge we have available to ourselves in Western medicine, but also trying to understand the entire milieu from which the patients come, and in which we come, too. It includes their spirituality, their beliefs, their feelings about life and death, their support groups, their families, their work and their home life. It has to do with all of it. It is what "healer" traditionally means—a person within the community, someone who is part of it. When I think of a medicine man, I think of a healer. It's the connotation that often comes to mind. A healer lives among the people; he is one of them, not separate from them.

In our world, it's not that way at all. Doctors live in a completely different society from the patients they care for. Who put them there? All of us did—doctors and patients, individually and working in concert. It incorporates the whole biomedical model, hardcore science, understanding the human being as a physiologic machine; and that incorporation creates a distancing. It divorces the physician from the idea of the mind, the soul and the spirit. All of those things are taken away until we convince ourselves that we are treating a machine in need of repair, not a human being in need of healing. If you start believing that, you don't feel connected any other way to the patient you're taking care of.

I once spoke to medical students who argued that the physician shouldn't get too close to the patient. They had heard this in some vague place, spoken by some vague person. They offered no specifics as to who imparted this rickety philosophy, but they were certain of its correctness. They had somehow come to believe that if you are going to adequately care for somebody, you can't get too close or you will lose your objectivity.

I countered that the problem is if you don't get close to your patients, you won't be able to treat them as whole people and you will see them only as a segment of what they really are, or more to the point, they become the segment you are treating—a heart valve, for instance.

As a medical student, an intern and a doctor, you are always going to face time pressures. They will be with you your whole lifetime. But time pressure is a poor excuse. At some point you have to confront the issue: Are you really listening to these people? Are you getting to the root of their problems?

Ultimately, that is what healers should do.

As the year moved along in fits and starts, I learned about disability, too, more than I ever dreamed. When insurance companies sell disability policies, they promise the world. Until the time actually comes that you suffer the misfortune of serious illness, you labor under the fantasy that the insurance company will be at your door begging you to take the money.

I am more than familiar with the cliché and even now sometimes shake my head at the naiveté that led to such a false sense of security. For this is when I learned about skeptical adjusters and private investigators sent to my home and office, people who combed every nook and cranny of my life, repeatedly questioning my honesty and character, certain that fraud lurked somewhere in the shadows of a "heart valve."

Physicians don't do well in recognizing the ramifications of disability, either. As a rule, doctors are workaholics and they believe this is how the rest of the world should operate, too. So the patient feels guilty when he says he doesn't know if he can go back to work yet. But none of this is black and white. There is no book with a chart that says "Aortic valve replacement— Takayasu's. Patient out of work X amount of time."

I did not know, either.

Should I be out three months, six months, a year? How do you gauge it? You think you should go by how you feel and that works to some degree, but there are so many variables that influence how you feel. What is your work? Is it physically demanding? Is it labor intensive? Or do you spend the day behind a desk? And even then, at what level of pressure?

Disability created anxiety I never anticipated. But by December, 1996, disability would slip into the background, a tangential concern to something much more pressing—survival.

On December 17, I decided to play volleyball on a Wednesday night. I missed the games and the companionship of the men who had been my close friends for so many years. I had been exercising and though I wasn't able to do as much as I could earlier in the year, I still felt strong enough to play.

We had just begun to play that night and I was standing on the court, waiting for play to continue. Suddenly, I was tired, out of breath and my heart beat rapidly.

I should have left the volleyball court, but I decided to keep going. I told myself I would take it easy and to some extent the decision was a success. The symptoms eased, but I played terribly the whole evening. My timing was off and I couldn't do anything right.

All these signs were telling me that I was going downhill again, that I was falling into deep trouble. I was frightened as I stood there on the court, but I kept playing.

Why? Pride. Stubbornness. I hadn't been there in months and I didn't want the other players to think I couldn't keep up. I kept telling myself that I could beat the illness. Even in the next two days, when I rode my bicycle near our home, I would push harder. It has always been my approach—*I'm going to beat this thing.*

In retrospect, it obviously would be correct to say my behavior was not wise. In my own defense, it was probably motivated out of fear, but also because I had been to what seemed like a million doctors and nobody told me anything was wrong. So if every one of them said everything was okay, what did I have to lose if I pushed myself harder?

My competitive nature arose. I didn't want to quit. I didn't want this thing to rule my life.

Had it not been for simple good luck three days after the volleyball game, it would have done more than rule my life. It would have ended it. I had gone for a routine examination by the rheumatologist. He listened to my heart and said, "Something's wrong."

CHAPTER NINE

When I looked down at the blood flowing from the deep cut between the thumb and forefinger of my right hand, no oracle suggested itself, nothing prophetic came to mind. I was worried about more pressing issues: bleeding and infection. Any suggestion of prophecy would come later.

It was early December and I had been building beds for the boys. Woodworking did something good for my soul. It was almost a form of therapy in itself and I wanted very much to finish the beds before the holidays.

This was going to be a big Christmas for us. We had much to celebrate. I had gone more than a year without any serious signs of progression of the Takayasu's. My medical practice had done well. We added two new nurse practitioners and another family practice physician to the staff. Beth's clinical research business was growing. We felt as if things had turned around.

The boys had been practicing for more than a month for their Christmas recitals. David played the piano and Andy the viola in the Junior Symphony; each was scheduled to play a solo at the Christmas Eve service at church. I enjoyed listening to them practice and always made a point of stopping whatever I was doing to spend time watching them. Whenever I saw Beth helping them through these practice times, I had the sense we would somehow get ourselves through whatever crises might arise. Along with that sense, came a heightened awareness of what I might lose.

I wrapped a towel around my bleeding hand and hurried to the telephone to call Beth. I knew of the potential for trouble when the saw blade ripped into my hand. Beth was at the mall and had not been gone long before I cut myself. I'm still not sure how it happened, though I suspect I had been working for so long in the cold garage that my hands became stiff and slipped as I was feeding a piece of wood into the saw blade.

I still was taking Coumadin, the blood thinner meant to prevent clotting. As I discovered, it also does a fine job of preventing normal coagulation when the skin is cut and blood begins to flow; and as any heart valve patient will attest, the second and more frightening prospect is that of infection. Before the day was out I started myself on oral antibiotics.

First, I needed to stop the bleeding, which I had not done by the time Beth returned home thirty minutes later. She answered her cell phone immediately when I called, but got caught in holiday mall traffic on the way home. I waited in the kitchen, my hand wrapped tightly in a blood-soaked towel. The cut gave no indication that it would stop bleeding on its own accord. The Coumadin was doing its work well.

It was about six o'clock by then and I didn't want to have to drive downtown to the Emergency Room. I called a friend and fellow volleyball player, Dr. Greg Pilette, an ER physician. He lived only a few minutes from us. Greg took one look at the cut and sent me on my way. It needed stitches.

Early on Sunday evening I expected the Emergency Room to be quiet. When I checked in to the triage area, the waiting room was filled with people—a girl in a wheelchair with an ice bag on her swollen ankle, a tired mother holding a flushed and coughing toddler, someone with a migraine, people with fevers and stomach aches. My hopes for a quick trip evaporated.

When I was finally called back to the treatment area, the nurse recognized me and apologized for the wait, explaining that they were short-staffed. I knew the ER doctor and we casually discussed holiday preparations and University of New Mexico basketball as he stitched up my lacerated hand.

When he was finished he said, "You know, you might want to take some antibiotics."

I told him I had already thought of it and had some at home. Neither of us could have known how significant a factor it would become. Three hours later, I was back home, no longer bleeding, still feeling optimistic about the coming Christmas, unaware that my stinging hand soon would be the least of my worries.

We were way ahead of schedule on everything. By the middle of the month we had not only decorated the tree, but bought all the gifts—the kids' stuff, our stuff, our friends' stuff, everything. We even managed to get them all wrapped and under the tree. As a rule we waited until the last minute on everything, with me being the role model for procrastination. I once left shopping for Beth's gift until Christmas Eve. When I finally broke away from the office, all of the stores were closed. There were no presents under the tree from me to Beth that year. But Beth received *very* nice gifts on the following Valentine's Day, Easter and Mother's Day.

I had been feeling tired the whole month. Coupled with the symptoms I had experienced at the volleyball game, I suppose I should not have been too surprised when my rheumatologist, Dr. Eddie Benge, lingered longer than usual with his stethoscope when he examined me. He had been seeing me every four to six weeks and the visits had become routine. This one would be the unwelcome exception to the rule.

My oldest son, Andy, went with me. He was 11 then and his school vacation had started the day before. We planned on going to a bookstore after my appointment with Dr. Benge. Andy was eager to spend some of his Christmas money on a new book and we were going to have breakfast together. We had been looking forward to it all week. After that I was going to drop Andy off at my parents' house and go from there to the office for our staff party.

When I spoke with Dr. Benge, I told him everything had been going well. I didn't mention anything about tiredness. This could have been oversight, but I believe I didn't say anything about my chronic tiredness for another reason: I had forgotten what it was like to feel normal. "Normal" for me had become a state of always being tired. If I was less tired than usual, that became feeling "good."

A second dilemma undergirded this change in self-assessment: How was I to properly assess my autoimmune symptoms? Was the tiredness a general symptom of the underlying heart disease or was it a symptom of deterioration? I preferred the less serious explanation.

As Dr. Benge listened to my heart, I knew it was taking longer than usual. I had nothing to measure this with other than the internal clock God gives to all of us, but I was certain he was taking too much time.

"I'm hearing a murmur," he said. "I want to get you over to the cardiologist's right now to get it checked out."

My mind began to run a little wild.

He called the cardiology office. Dr. Paul Cochran wasn't there, but the cardiologist on call was available.

I couldn't believe this was happening again.

I had to do something with Andy. I didn't want him to have to sit around and wait and get scared. I told Dr. Benge I would go to the cardiologist's as soon I dropped off my son.

On the freeway, I could not rid myself of the thought of another heart surgery. I did not want to do this again. I tried to diagnose the problem myself, always a mistake for a doctor in any case but particularly fruitless in this case. There was no point to it, yet I did it anyway, almost reflexively.

At the cardiology office, they got me back into the examining room quickly. An echocardiogram was done and as luck would have it, just as the procedure was wrapping up, Dr. Cochran, my regular cardiologist and still on vacation, just happened to stop in at the office. He stayed to view the echocardiogram. The news was not good. The valve itself was not leaking, but the area around the valve was. He wanted me back in the hospital and he did not mean later that day or that evening or first thing next morning. He meant now. He gave me enough time to make the short trip to my office so I could tell Beth in person, but after that he wanted me back in Presbyterian for more tests.

Following this announcement, there came yet another "patient moment" for me, another door opening so I might view medicine from a different perspective.

Dr. Cochran was still on vacation. He said he would not be working over the weekend and that another doctor would be seeing me. He said he would return the following Monday. As a patient, I would have preferred that he was there; as a patient, I wanted him to work on the weekend he had planned to take off. I had a lot of confidence in him that I didn't have in the other doctor. I trusted Dr. Cochran implicitly. Not only was he skilled and experienced, he was also down to earth and, most important, he listened. I had bonded with him. He had guided me through the first surgery and my recovery. I believed in him and I did not want anyone else, though I never said anything to him about it. As a doctor, I knew that the time he had set aside for himself was valuable. In my own practice, I had worked hard at preserving my time away from work, but even with this effort, the practice continually eroded free time. I had seen too many overworked physicians burn out because they were not able to establish a boundary between their patients and their lives outside of medicine.

Thoughts of time balancing dissolved as soon as I walked into my clinic office. My eyes met Beth's. I didn't have to say a word.

We went into the office and closed the door. I told her what happened and she cried. So did I. We held one another for a long time, rocking back and forth, not wanting to let go. Each of us found strength and safety in the other's embrace. Letting go started the nightmare all over again. It was as though we were trying to stave off the inevitable.

Beth said, "It's not fair. It's just not fair."

Often, I have wondered how many of my patients lived through moments like that, moments now seared into my mind but at best only an abstraction before I lived them, and certainly not anything I might have brought up with a patient in an examining room.

I don't know how long Beth and I stayed like that, locked in a protective, futile embrace. Eventually, she began to shift into what I have always called her take-charge mode. In a crisis, she has an ability to detach from the emotional aspects which allows her to assess a situation and think things through. Everything about her—her voice, her body language—suggests that things will be all right if everyone will just settle down and take one step at a time. It's almost as if her demeanor is a language in its own right.

The next step would be to tell the staff.

When we opened the door, they were gathered in the hallway near my office. They had heard us and they were all crying too. It was the day of the office Christmas party. We already had ordered the food and decorated the office. I was going to give out the bonus checks and we were going to celebrate. I told them to go ahead with the party and that I would be okay. Later, they said they went through the motions, but the party was more like a wake.

Beth called friends who contacted everyone in our church fellowship group. My mother picked up David up from school. David's reaction mirrored Beth's. "It's not fair," he said.

Beth and I had many long conversations about the idea of fairness, all of them contingent on where we might be on the Takayasu's continuum at the time. It is human nature to ask, "Why is this happening to me?" when a crisis of this magnitude visits itself upon a life. It is almost always the first visceral reaction to a shattering blow. There were times when I felt we were being punished. I asked myself, "What did we do wrong? What did we do to deserve this? What didn't we get the first time around?"

Of course, there were no rational answers to these questions.

My initial defense against the onslaught of the disease was to square off against it and spit in its eye. When we were able to step back from it, Beth and I returned to our religious faith, our belief in God's plan. It enabled us to hang on. Even when faced with the nightmare of illness, we believed there had to be some reason for it, regardless of our inability to understand it.

When not considering these spiritual and philosophical questions, we found ourselves dealing with more secular ones I am tempted to call mundane were it not for my inattention to the obvious. Incredible as it seems to me now, I did not have a will or a durable power of attorney. Like so many other men and women our age, perhaps we had succumbed unconsciously to the fairy tale of immortality. Others might tragically die young. Not us.

Beth and I had been telling each other for months that we had to get the will done. It should have been one of our first priorities after my recovery. In our medical careers, we had been involved in many difficult ethical dilemmas with patients because they had not left such directives. We used to shake our heads sadly (and sagely, I'm sure) while talking about how much anguish could be spared if people would only make provisions for situations like this. Beth and I had talked about it frequently and we were clear about what the other's wishes would be in the event of a bad outcome. But that would not be enough. We had seen too many examples of families overruled by institutions and courts in decisions involving their loved ones.

Now, finally, we would tend to this unpleasant, important task. Two attorneys in the fellowship group had offered to help any way they could. We called them and they set about having a will drawn up. Beth drove me to the hospital and I checked in, a veteran patient now—clothes off, gown on, blood drawn—all of it too familiar. That afternoon, the attorneys came with the will and other documents: a Durable Power of Attorney, an Advanced Health Care Directive. We signed the documents with heavy hearts. It was one of the hardest moments we experienced during this hospitalization. If not outright capitulation to the inevitable, it was concrete evidence of what could happen. Until we held the pens in our hands and prepared to sign the papers, the prospect of mortality could be deflected. Had I been in my 70s instead of my 40s, perhaps I would have looked death more squarely in the eye.

Beth went back to the office to arrange for coverage of my patients by other doctors and to reschedule her clinical trial patients for the next week.

The infectious disease doctor on call came into my room at some point in the afternoon.

He was young and in his first year out of residency. I didn't know him. In view of my recent hand injury, he wanted to start IV antibiotic therapy right after blood cultures could be obtained. I knew that my hand injury could have been the source of the problem and an infection could have set up in the valve causing significant damage.

Later, the blood cultures came back negative. This did not necessarily mean there was no infection present because I had been on antibiotics for the hand injury. A decision was made to keep me on the IV antibiotics "just to be safe."

Later that afternoon, the covering cardiologist came in and said she had to do another Trans-Esophageal Echocardiogram.

I knew it was the diagnostic test of choice because it is the most sensitive for detecting infection on the valve, but I nonetheless shuddered at the prospect of having to undergo it again.

She seemed oblivious to my distress. She was curt and displayed little emotion or compassion at all, reinforcing my belief that doctors should undergo many of the tests to which they routinely subject their patients.

Just after the cardiologist made clear what the rules of the game were, Beth returned and came to my bedside. The cardiologist's body language, underscored with a brief, irritated glance at Beth, made it clear that she viewed Beth's presence as nothing less than an interruption. It was as if two people had walked into the room—I saw a loved one; the physician saw an irritant. She turned her back to Beth and continued telling me what she was going to do.

The only words that passed between the physician and my wife came when the technician arrived with the TEE equipment.

"You will have to go now," the doctor abruptly said to Beth.

The tech gave me an embarrassed look and shrugged.

Those were the only words the doctor spoke to Beth the entire weekend. While doing rounds over the course of those two days, the cardiologist checked on me four or five times. Beth was always with me. The doctor never spoke to her. Not a word.

Banished to the hallway for the duration of the test, Beth paced, understandably worried about me. When the test was finished, the physician barged out of the room and brushed by Beth, again not saying a word.

So instead of a clear, authoritative explanation of the results coming from the cardiologist who conducted the test, Beth heard the results from me, still groggy from the sedative. She was visibly upset because the cardiologist clearly had not talked to her, but instead talked *down* to her. For the first time in all of our contacts with medicine from the patient's perspective, a physician ordered Beth to leave the room when it came time to do the procedure. It was a textbook example of how not to treat a patient and his loved ones. ("Textbook" actually may be too kind. "Caricature" would be more accurate.)

The cardiologist told me I had a leak around the valve. The valve itself seemed to be seated well, but I was leaking all around it. We would later find out that the valve was wobbling, barely doing its job.

The mechanical valve has a ring around it and typically what the surgeon does is sew that ring into the aortic root tissue. In my case, they had sewed into the portion of aortic tissue that remained when they removed the valve the previous year. Apparently, the stitches were no longer there or had loosened and the tissue never adhered to the valve ring as it should have.

I was admitted to the hospital on Friday at 11 A.M. and discharged on Tuesday, Christmas Eve, at 4:45 P.M. I saw the usual contingent of consultants and doctors, though many were covering doctors and I did not have the same rapport with them. It was the Christmas holidays and many of the regular doctors had taken time off. The hospital probably was quieter in some ways. Many elective surgeries are not done in those final weeks of December because the doctors are gone or the patients want to wait until after the holidays.

The two doctors most involved in my case that weekend were young and fresh out of their medical specialty fellowship. Beth and I had no confidence in them, though their age and inexperience had little to do with our qualms. They had acquired an all too common arrogance, a superiority with no substance meant to function as a cover, a defensive mechanism to shield them from what they didn't know. My attempts to discuss my condition and possible treatments and outcomes with them were met with indifference. We had to sit tight and wait for Dr. Cochran to come back on Monday.

The window of my room faced north. Our church, First Presbyterian, was directly across the highway from the hospital. On Sunday morning, we watched the people coming and going from the church. Members of our TGIF group looked up toward our window on the seventh floor and waved. Almost all of them had visited over the weekend and knew which room I was in. We knew they would be praying for me.

There were not many patients in the cardiac unit that weekend and the nurses had more time to spend with us. Our good luck with the CCU "census" was exactly the kind of thing that causes hospital administrators to generate endless memos on cost-effectiveness.

Hospital administrations see healthcare delivery as "business." The bottom line is profit. Nursing is the biggest money losing department in the hospital and their approach is to get the job done with as few nurses as possible. This results in an emphasis on tasks instead of seeing the patient as a whole person. Care is fragmented. Short staffing is the norm.

When the patient census is low, nurses get to do what they went into nursing to do—comfort and care for the sick. They have the time to answer anxious questions and explain what they are doing.

They get a chance to ask, "Would you like to talk?"

They get a chance to ask, "How do you feel about this?"

They get a chance to say, "I'm so sorry about what is happening to you."

They have the time to put their arms around you. They have the time to laugh and cry with you. This is what happened to us that weekend before Christmas.

Monday morning finally arrived and with it Dr. Paul Cochran. He seemed surprised that a cardiac catheterization had not yet been performed, saying that the procedure would yield necessary information about the nature and severity of my valve problem and that it would be of vital importance to the cardiac surgeons.

He scheduled the procedure for early the next morning. It was at this time that he first suggested I go out of state to have the second heart surgery done because no one in Albuquerque was familiar enough with the highly specialized procedure now required. He straightforwardly told me he just wasn't comfortable having the work done here.

My first reaction to his suggestion was most un-physician like. *How can I do this?* I thought. *I don't want to leave my family and the comfort of familiar surroundings. I think I'll just stay here.*

I was not even sure I knew exactly what had to be done. Like patients who are frightened or who are having to process too much information (and often information presented in alien medical tongues), you don't quite hear everything said to you, even if you think you are paying attention.

I am a physician, I understand the language spoken by physicians, I have had hundreds of these conversations with my colleagues. But I didn't hear everything Dr. Cochran said. I didn't catch on right away to just how extensive this surgery would be.

Given my status as a medical professional, this makes no sense, but the fact of the matter is at that moment I wasn't a doctor; I was a scared, confused patient, trying to right my upside-down world. I was centered on illogical thoughts of staying close to home, not on the medical ramifications being explained to me.

I asked my nurse to request that someone from the cardiac surgery team come to talk with me when they came to the unit. I was hoping to speak to one of the cardiovascular surgeons who had been involved with my previous surgery. As luck would have it, the first member of the team to come by that day was the one who reopened my chest in a torturous, medieval fashion only the year before.

Unlike Dr. Cochran, he was quite sure they could do everything I would need in Albuquerque. No questions, no doubts, no hesitation—which did nothing to instill confidence. If any-thing, his hubris sent a message clearly opposite of what he intended.

On that Monday, December 23, at five o'clock in the after-noon, there occurred an event I still have trouble grasping in its fullness. Perhaps it is beyond any human being's capacity to understand all of its implications. To say it was spiritual is correct but inadequate; to say it was the most moving expression of love and community I have experienced in my life is equally correct and equally inadequate.

Our fellowship group had organized a prayer circle for me. As they did with the first one during my surgery in the summer, they gathered in the hospital chapel. But this prayer circle came with a difference: I was there to witness it, and I will be forever grate-ful that God allowed me to do so.

With IV poles trailing behind me and friends and family clearing the way through the hospital's corridors, my wheelchair entourage made quick work of the trip from my CCU room to the chapel. When we arrived, I could not believe the scene that unfolded before me. My hospitalization had been announced at the church service on Sunday. The chapel was filled with people—our pastor, my parents, my patients, people from out-side the TGIF group, adults, children.

Paul Debenport, our pastor, opened with a prayer and then asked each person in the chapel to go around the room to speak or offer prayers. The people present poured out their hearts in expressions of faith, joy and love. Sometimes preceding their remarks with a moment's meditation, each person opened up sincerely. There was a tangible connection between us. Everyone spoke through tears. I do not know how to describe this, except to say there was an eternal dimension to this gath-ering and I did not doubt God's presence in that room for one second. It was a powerful communion of the deepest fellowship and love. It will live in my heart and soul always. It was a privileged moment.

The people who had not been involved with our group until that point marveled at the depth of the connection we shared. My parents, who had been devoted churchgoers all of their lives, said they had never seen or felt anything like it. Afterward, we lingered in the chapel. No one wanted to leave the sanctuary. Beth and I stayed for half an hour.

The next day, I spoke with another member of the surgery group, Dr. Diane Sansonetti, a fine doctor I had long held in the highest regard. She is known for getting to the point quickly and she did not disappoint in this case. She agreed with Dr. Cochran. I needed to leave town for the surgery.

"I don't think we've done enough of these procedures to be comfortable," she said. "We may have done one or two on an emergency basis, but we've done none otherwise."

Two physicians for whom I had the greatest respect now echoed one another. It was to be a Medical Center in California, where I would come under the care of a renowned heart surgeon. Everything Dr. Sansonetti and Dr. Cochran said made sense. It had to be this way.

Even so, I wasn't ready to give up the fight. That my resistance to leaving Albuquerque flew in the face of common sense and medical expertise I trusted did little to slow me down. I had other ideas. I look back at them now in amazement.

When I was able to speak to my family about the prospect of surgery in California, I thought they would be on *my* side, whatever that might have been. I hoped to hear, "Oh, you don't have to go. They can do it here." But I didn't hear anything of the kind.

Beth said, "Yeah, you ought to go."

My brother said, "When do we leave?"

My parents said if that's what it takes, I should do it.

How could they not see what I saw: *It's warm here, it's fuzzy here, I like it here, I don't want to leave.*

The tide was gaining momentum and I surrendered. I was going to California. The question then became when.

Dr. Cochran was reluctant to let me go home. He felt it would be prudent to stay in the Albuquerque hospital until the time came to fly to California. I begged him to allow me to go home for Christmas. He could see how desperately Beth and I wanted to be home with the children before facing the uncertainty of what awaited us far from home.

My lobbying paid off. He agreed against his better judgment that if I tolerated the heart cath and post-op procedures (which were six hours long), then I could be discharged.

There is no doubt in my mind that had I not been a doctor and Beth a nurse, we would have been observing Christmas in the hospital. Call it what you will—professional courtesy, pulling rank, an insider's perk—I was prepared to do whatever it took to spend Christmas with my sons and Beth.

Dr. Cochran performed the cardiac catheterization the next morning. About three o'clock that afternoon, he came up to the room to see how I was doing before making the final decision about allowing me to go home. I could tell he was still reluctant to let me go.

My lobbying descended to begging. We threw ourselves at the feet of his considerable compassion.

It was Christmas Eve. My oldest son, Andy, was to play a viola solo in a special children's service; my younger son, David, would be playing the piano. Andy was playing one of the Three Wise Men in the re-enactment of the birth of Christ. We had attended this early evening Christmas Eve service every year since moving to New Mexico the year Andy was born. We desperately wanted to be there.

Dr. Cochran relented. He agreed to let me go. We were jubilant. He was worried.

Beth and I would always be grateful to him for the gift of that Christmas. The nurses told us they never had an inpatient discharged the day of a catheterization, and certainly not one in my condition.

Beth bundled up as many of the things that needed to be taken home as she could carry, ran out of the hospital and drove home to change clothes and pick up everyone at the house. Back at the hospital, the nurses helped me pack up. Beth had brought my suit to the hospital that morning in hopes that we would be going home, so I was ready for the one-block trip to the church as soon as she returned. When she pulled into the doctors' parking lot, a nurse was pushing me in a wheelchair through the door. All the remaining flowers and personal items were piled in my lap.

The nurse had stayed with me in the hospital room, keeping watch from the window for Beth. As soon as we saw her turn the corner from the freeway exit, we left. We reached the doctors entrance to the hospital at the same time.

Anyone familiar with how long it usually takes to get a patient out of the hospital once he has been discharged will understand why the episode looked like a jail break.

It took no more than a minute to drive from the hospital to the church. I limped in, walking straight-legged because I was not supposed to bend my leg at the hip any more than I had to in order to prevent reopening the puncture wound in my groin. I was weak and I put my arm around Beth's shoulder for support.

We entered the sanctuary five minutes before the service started. When we walked in, the entire congregation stood to greet us. Our friends and family came forward and crowded around us, giving us hugs and congratulating me. We settled into the first pew and the service began.

The beauty of the sanctuary and the ritual of the children's service comforted me. I held Beth's hand throughout the service and listened to the story of Christmas with a humble heart. For a precious hour I sat there, suffused in the warmth of these loving people. But the moment was short-lived.

After the service, we went to my parents' house, a Christmas Eve tradition. I sat in the living room, practically mute, feeling isolated and distant. We left early and came home.

Our street was softly lit by row after row of New Mexico's Christmastime magic—*luminarias*—small paper bags with a lighted candle inside resting in a base of sand. They are meant to light the way for the Christ child and as always, all of our neighbors had lined the streets and driveways with them.

Our house had none. For the first time in seven years, our house was dark on Christmas Eve.

Every Christmas Eve, Beth and I sat together in front of the tree late into the night, reminiscing about things that had happened that year and retelling stories of earlier Christmases. Beth would turn out all the lights except the ones on the tree while I poured two Irish cremes. Then we sat on the couch, watching the tree lights twinkle and remembering the stories that went with each of the ornaments we had collected over the years. Sometimes we would be exhausted, wrapping gifts until two or three in the morning. On those nights, all we wanted to do was crawl into bed for a couple of hours' sleep before the boys woke us before dawn, but when Beth put the last present under the tree, I always found another moment to fill the two small glasses and sit with her.

After the boys were born, our talks centered more around what we wanted for the future. We marveled at how fast Andy and David were growing up and how proud of them we were. Sometimes we talked about what we wanted to do after the boys left home and how we imagined it would be for us to grow old together.

That Christmas Eve there was no talk about the future. I stretched out on the couch while Beth put the gifts under the tree and stuffed the stockings. Then we turned out all of the lights and went to bed. We lay there quietly, holding hands, not speaking, until we finally drifted off to sleep.

We got up early and the kids raced around. I sat in a chair, an observer, not a participant.

My world kept going, but I was no longer a part of it. Christmas had an air of unreality. We had hinted about canceling the family dinner at our house. Everyone was tense and tired, but we continued on in something of a family tradition: When in crisis go about business as usual. It made it easier to pretend everything was okay. Our hints about canceling the dinner fell on deaf ears. My mother told Beth it was important to make sure that things were kept as normal as possible. Beth and her mother spent the day cooking the enormous dinner they had planned weeks before.

People dropped by to visit. None of it seemed authentic to me; I didn't seem to be there. The distancing that had begun with my descent into illness created another dimension in which I now lived. I went through the motions, the smiles and handshakes, the holiday greetings, the dinner conversation. It all seemed a charade, something to paper over the gulf separating two very different universes.

We left for California three days after Christmas, but not before one more bit of enlightenment came into my life. I had long thought airlines made special arrangements for people with medical emergencies. To my dismay, I found there is no such thing. Airlines had no policy we could discover that addressed the kind of medical situation I was in.

I do not remember a sadder moment in my life then when I walked into the Albuquerque airport. My sons were at home. When I kissed them good-bye, I clung to the hope that I would come back and see them. But I just didn't know. The boys had spent the morning walking around with their heads down, not speaking much, if at all. They knew what was going on. They had been through it once before. I am not sure if the younger one knew how close to death I was, but I am certain his older brother had a very good understanding of the situation and was trying to be brave about it.

Beth's mother had come to visit over the holidays, arriving the day I was admitted to the hospital, yet another example of how illness has a way of disrupting the best laid plans. She was able to stay for another week so the kids would be home in familiar surroundings. Friends were more than willing to take in the kids, but it was so much better that they would be with their grandmothers.

To this day it saddens me to think about leaving my sons and wondering if I would ever see them again. It is a sadness shared many times over by parents confronting a similar loss and it would go undiscussed in the next few days at the California Medical Center. No one would ask about the pain of a father thinking that as he walked out the front door of his home it might very well be the last time he saw his children. No one would ask about the crushing stresses that slowly suffocated two parents and two young boys. No one would inquire about the effect of such strain on the patient's health.

For the next few days I would not be a parent or a husband or a doctor. My identity had been established at the Medical Center long before I arrived.

I was a "redo."

We landed in California around five o'clock in the afternoon. I don't remember much about the flight. I was getting progressively weaker. The disease was moving along quickly now.

CHAPTER TEN

Walking through the airport, I made it only a few yards at a time before I had to stop to rest. Everything in my life now seemed to move in slow motion. Beth and I had reversed roles and I chafed at the continual reminders that I not only had to be waited on, but had to stand by and watch her do everything, too. She got me into my seat and put the carry-on luggage in the overhead bin. During the flight, she helped set up my meal tray, pulled the lid off the juice container and opened the plastic packet that contained the condiments.

The simplest task required an effort I no longer could mount. I rode most of the way with my eyes closed, but I didn't sleep. It wasn't so much that I was tired as it was not having the strength to keep my eyes open. We had upgraded to first class for the comfort, but it made little difference. The illness had begun to take on new dimensions and I knew it.

Everything was ready in anticipation of our arrival at the Medical Center's Guest House, a much-welcomed refuge for patients and families. It was owned by the Medical Center and run as a nonprofit organization. With its mission-style furnishings and lovely architecture, everything in the facility, down to the smallest detail, was designed to create tranquility—art, pottery, photographs, fabric wall hangings, Japanese flower arrangements. The soft-spoken attendants at the registration desk dressed in navy blue uniforms were pleasant but not patronizing. A friend and fellow physician who lived nearby brought in her high tech coffee maker, a grinder, coffee, tea and enough gourmet food of every description to last for weeks.

Once established in the room, we decided to take a walk. It was around nine o'clock in the evening and a popular deli was only a few blocks away. Our walk was all downhill, but by the time we got to the deli, I was exhausted and glad to sit down in a booth to rest. We ordered one of my favorite desserts. Normally, I would have been delighted to see it on the menu, but I ate only a few bites. On the walk back to the Guest House, I struggled. I didn't feel short of breath, but I was tired and we stopped frequently so I could rest.

When we got back, I fell asleep immediately. The next day (Sunday) Beth and I again tried to walk around the immediate neighborhood, but it was an exercise in futility and frustration. We had gone only blocks and I was worn out.

That afternoon, we checked in at the Medical Center. Huge, spread out, monolithic, severe—it left no doubt about its nature and purpose when you walked in. It is a Medical Center befitting the metropolis that surrounds it.

We filled out the consent forms, insurance forms, and other paperwork, then went up to the cardio-thoracic unit, where someone told us we were in luck. I had requested a private room and it just so happened that the hospital recently had remodeled a section of the unit. I would be the first person in it.

I do not mean to be ungrateful, as I recall the unit's staff being kind and helpful, but if my room had just been remodeled, I hate to think what the previous occupant might have seen before the improvement. At best, the room was sterile. One lonely picture hung on the wall, a sad, generic landscape with green hills, trees, and flowers that would have been right at home in a Howard Johnson's. The walls had been painted an all too familiar institutional green. It was not the olive drab of an Army barracks, but a pale washed out green, a decorator's idea of pastel.

The room came with a view of a solid brick wall, a muddy, reddish brown. From my bed, I looked out and could see nothing living, though if I got out of the bed and walked to the window and looked directly down, a courtyard spread out below.

Another window afforded a uniquely California vista—earthquake damage not yet repaired. We asked the staff about it and they pointed out obvious cracks in the bricks and places where sizeable chunks had fallen out altogether. The California earthquake veterans spoke about their geologic phenomenon in the casual way a New Mexican might mention a dry arroyo turned into a treacherous flash flood by a summer storm racing across the high desert.

Then it was down to the business of being a patient again.

Off with your clothes, on with the gown. Off with your dignity, off with your individuality, off with any outward expression of who you might be, as you give away a part of yourself to the monolith with a view of earthquake damage. In only minutes, you don the uniform and mindset that identifies your caste, the repeated capitulations to the system eventually causing you to identify with Charlie Chaplin, squished in the gears of "Modern Times." Chaplin becomes more and more apt as you are swept along a hospital conveyor belt that stops only after your surrender becomes unconditional.

The unit was short-staffed that afternoon. The nurse assigned to me knew Beth was also a nurse and asked if Beth wanted to start my IV. The nurse said it would be of great help if Beth would do so. This was highly irregular and Beth declined. (IV insertion was a painful procedure for me. The Takayasu's had toughened my veins and the Teflon IV catheters crumpled like straws when they met the resistance.)

Another nurse shaved me, yet one more exercise in exposure and surrender endured by patients everywhere. Here's a woman shaving my groin area, and, to borrow a word from my teen-age son, it's weird. Stimulating in ways, which is bizarre, humiliating in other ways, which is only humiliating. She does everything possible to be clinical about it while shaving an area fraught with deep-seated meaning, but from the patient's point of view, "clinical" is not an idea that springs to mind.

Yet one more time I found myself thinking that I never really understood the implications of all this until I experienced it myself. I knew it intellectually. I understood it (or thought I did) on some formal, abstract level. I had seen hundreds of patients go through it and it should have been second nature to me. But in truth, I understood nothing. It was reminiscent of my experience with Beth when we met at the White Mountain Reservation in Arizona. Neither of us had been a parent then, and yet we felt quite comfortable conducting parenting classes based on brochures and studies. It was not until our sons were born that we discovered we knew nothing about parenting.

Half an hour after the nurse left, the chief resident walked in. He had come to talk about the procedure and from the moment he appeared in the doorway, I had a bad feeling about him.

He presented me with a consent form and said, "You have to sign this."

"What about the surgeon?" I said. "When do I get to talk to him?"

Uncertainty flickered across the chief resident's eyes.

"Okay," he said in a way that made it clear this part of the conversation was over as far he was concerned.

He slipped the consent form back on his clipboard, did a quick history on me, checked me physically (giving new meaning to the word "indifference") and left.

Minutes later another doctor came in. He was young, an intern in his first year out of medical school. He sang the second verse of the same song begun by the chief resident. He carried himself in such a way as to suggest that arrogance might be a good thing and superciliousness a merit badge. His body language announced the divide between our stations in life and that he had no intention of trying to bridge it. He was the doctor, I was the patient, and he entertained no notion of lowering himself to my level so we might converse as equals, one human being to another. He said he had to do my history and write my orders. He sat down in a chair, looking as if he were prepared to wield his clipboard like a club.

"First, I need to know—"

I held up my hand to stop him.

"What exactly is your position in all this?" I said. "How do you fit into this team?"

He looked at me as if I were his first patient from Mars. This was a young doctor, but it was clear he was not accustomed to being questioned by the patient caste.

"By the way, I'm Dr. Hsi," I said.

This information seemed to confuse him. It muddled what heretofore had been a well-drawn battlefield. But he was game for one more try. He drew another weapon—the surgical consent form, apparently handed off to him by the recently departed chief resident. He waved the consent form in my direction and said I must sign it. I told him I didn't think it would be a good idea for me to sign the release until after I had spoken with the surgeon.

He seemed taken aback. My refusal had destroyed his protocol and he didn't know what to do about it.

I asked more questions. He gave few answers simply because he had only few to give. He was not in a position to provide answers. He was an intern, a rookie, the most powerless position in the medical hierarchy. Yet he had adopted the "attitude" already. I wondered where it came from. Who taught him this? In the vast system of medical training in California or the entire United States for that matter, how did this bright young man come to believe that the proper way to treat a patient was with disdain?

He backed down a little bit, which is what I wanted him to do, because he shouldn't treat anyone the way he was treating me, a patient facing heart surgery in less than twelve hours. I wanted him to know my position and that I wasn't going to sit there and acquiesce to his assumption that I was something less than an equal in our exchange.

None of this set the stage for a good working relationship with him. Because I teach resident medical students at the University of New Mexico, I was hoping that it might be an opportunity to educate him a little bit, but I don't believe he was educable at that point. He became offended and it was obvious to me that it was not a good teaching moment. Beth, on the other hand, thought it was great.

In the next two hours, four more people came in and asked questions I had already answered many times, but I had become weary of the parade and I don't recall who they were or why they came.

Between interrogators, I tried to imagine what my chart might say:

(A) 41-year-old, Asian-American, male, physician
(B) Status Post: St. Jude's valve replacement and Teflon graft 6/95
(C) Diagnosis: Takayasu's aortitis
(D) Now admitted for redo due to pseudoaneurysm and loosening of the valve.
(E) Plan: Surgery

This is how we learn to be precise in our talk of patients. We then describe a little bit of the history, medications and anything else that is relevant. It is the kind of story you will see on any patient who comes to this Medical Center or anywhere else. And yes, it is precise, but it strikes me as so lacking in any suggestion of humanness. We have truly broken down this individual into the few components that matter, but nowhere in there is any mention made of a patient's life. I wanted to be treated as a human being, not as a disease. I wanted someone to sit down and talk *to* me, not *at* me.

Doctors have already made up their minds about what is going to happen before they go into that hospital room. When they enter the room, it is not to ask the patient any questions, certainly not to ask "What do you think we can do to help you?" They come in only to tell the patient what will happen, to explain judgments and rulings already made. The decision about what was going to happen to me had been made before I got to the Medical Center. What I wanted to know was if someone was going to at least listen to me a little. Would there be anyone the least bit interested in knowing who I was?

They would be asking me to place my life in their hands, and if you are going to give people that much power, you want them to have a modicum of concern about who you are as an individual. It would take only a few minutes to make that connection with the patient and once made it gives the patient a greater sense that the person who is going to be operating on him cares about who he is and that he will not be looked upon only as one more machine to be tuned up.

As a group, physicians sometimes forget what the business is all about. They forget about the humanity that is involved. It is a way of being concise and brief and there certainly is a time and place for that. I would never argue otherwise. If they are in a huddle outside my room and talking about a valve redo, that's fine. They need to do that. But I do not need to hear it. (In actuality, they did not bother with the formal adjective to describe the "redo." I was not a "valve redo." I was just the "redo.")

The charge nurse from the cardio-thoracic intensive care unit came in to visit. In a nursing unit's hierarchy there is the head nurse, who is responsible for the unit on all three shifts and the three charge nurses who run the individual shifts. The day shift charge nurse is the most important. She makes the assignments, coordinates the varied responsibilities and requirements and makes sure things run smoothly. Part of her job was to see all the pre-op patients scheduled for admission to her unit the next day. At the Medical Center she would meet pre-op patients so they would see a familiar face later on. I am sure it was intended as an attempt to counterbalance the prevailing impersonal climate.

"You're the redo scheduled for 8 A.M., right?" she said.

I heard the same word from the "patient advocate." I was the redo.

In terms of efficiency and precision, an argument can be made for the use of jargon in any field, but efficiency is not improved when used as a device to cancel out the "bother" of treating patients as whole human beings rather than a disparate collection of broken parts. Some of the most compassionate physicians are the best physicians. I would argue that the most compassionate make sure they are doing the best possible job. Somewhere in the back of their minds, something is telling them this is a father, this is a husband, and by God I want to do my best to make sure this person can go back to doing the things that matter in his life.

Is this too much to ask of a physician?

I have heard exactly that contention from medical students—yes, they say, it is too much—and I will argue against the notion forever. What is our job if we don't take on some of these things emotionally? If we can't handle the emotional levels of illness and dying, then we aren't in the right business and probably more suited to be auto mechanics.

When the parade of clipboards and questions finally ended, we decided Thai food might help our spirits. One of the hospital neighborhood's greatest attributes was an abundance of good ethnic restaurants. Those restaurants became a routine for Beth and family and friends. Whenever I was hospitalized, they would get take-out from an Asian restaurant. We were in the middle of one of those happy food moments when the reverie was cut short by the entrance of the surgeon who would perform my surgery. It was around 9 P.M. Five other surgeons trailed into the room behind him.

He was a slight man with a long thin face and deep-set eyes. He wore a starched, white lab coat with his name embroidered in blue on the pocket; a regimental tie complemented an Oxford shirt. He didn't strike me as the kind of guy who would do rounds in his scrubs. He had a commanding presence, so much so that when he walked in a room, a hush fell over whatever space may be within reach of that presence. Only later would a friend and fellow physician who knew him tell us that he was commonly referred to as "God" in the Medical Center.

He introduced his colleagues quickly, rattling off names as if he were reciting a grocery list. Without ever physically leaving the room, the other doctors seemed to disappear in it. Two of them leaned against a wall, obviously very tired. While the heart surgeon spoke, they never looked up; I never made eye contact with them. The others hung back when he stepped forward to my bed.

He asked me how the plane ride from Albuquerque had been, demonstrating a style I would become familiar with as I knew him better. He started every conversation with some kind of formal, perfunctory question. It seemed to be understood that responses were expected to be brief and that extended conversation was not a possibility.

He said he would be operating on me and asked how I was feeling. I told him about my extreme fatigue and shortness of breath after exertion, but he showed little interest in any of the events that led up to my arrival at the Medical Center, though he did say he'd spoken with my cardiologist and that he was familiar with the situation.

He explained the procedure, and I cannot rid myself of the sense that the presentation was canned, that it had been given in the past just as I was hearing it now and that it would be given the same way again in the future. In the next room or the room across the hall or two rooms down, the recitation's words would not vary much from patient to patient, the common denominator a rote efficiency that certainly was medically correct and, by design or not, capable of performing double duty—its precision created distance.

He said the surgeons would put in an artificial conduit with the artificial valve incorporated within and that they would sew it to the ventricle itself. They would take out the aortic root. They would do what is known as a modified Bentall procedure in which the aortic root is removed and the coronary arteries are sewn back into the conduit. There was about a 14 percent risk of mortality and in my case probably a little less because I was younger and in pretty good health otherwise.

About that time in his presentation, a phenomenon for which I have no explanation asserted itself. Suddenly, it seemed that everyone on my side of the room was struck dumb, unable to speak, unable to formulate questions, unable to do anything but stand by, passive and mute.

Sorry to say, I include myself in this silent group.

With the exception of my mother, all of us were medical professionals—me, my wife the former ICU nurse, my brother the pediatrician, our friend the physician and Medical Center staff member. We had spent a good deal of the day discussing questions in anticipation of the surgeon's arrival. But as soon as he walked through the door, it was as if our collective brain had shut down.

Questions? What questions? We didn't have any.

All I could think was here is a surgeon whom I've flown all the way from Albuquerque to see and who will do a life-and-death operation on me tomorrow and he is telling me I have a 14 percent chance of mortality and he knows virtually nothing about who I am.

I looked around the room to see if any of the residents or other doctors who came in with him picked up on what was going on. Somehow I wanted someone to show a spark of understanding, some hint of compassion. I saw nothing of the kind. Instead, I saw myself in them. I saw my long days and sleepless nights in medical school. We followed along with an attending physician and it was assumed that we would not interject any of our own commentary. We would listen only. Never speaking while in the patient's room, we might talk about the case later down the hall but even those conversations were held in accordance with the hierarchy. If you were an intern, the chances were you would not talk much at all; if you were a resident, you might be able to ask a few questions, though with a resident there is an assumption that you should know what's going on.

What I remember most is that you are tired.

You walk in the room and see the human being in the bed as a procedure or a disease. With no effort at all you stop thinking of him as an individual. I routinely did it as a resident and it appalled me now to see it from the patient's point of view. When I was the object of this ingrained depersonalization, it distressed me greatly. It brought back memories of when I was a chronically tired resident just trying to get through the day with the patient's needs never entering the equation.

I don't know why medicine is taught this way. Perhaps it is because residents are the ones who have to oversee the day-to-day care of patients. They write the orders, visit the patients, do the surgeries. They have to build in the time between these duties to write reports, orders and meet with other doctors, all of which eats up enormous amounts of time. It is assumed that unless you spend sixteen or twenty hours a day in the hospital, you are not working hard enough. Part of it might be an initiation process, part of it nothing more than habit; it has been this way for years and no one has found a way to do it differently.

It is true to some degree that the more hours you spend in a hospital the more you see and the more you end up doing, but there is a point of diminishing returns that suggests we run a serious risk of damaging patients, perhaps even fatally. At the very least, one of the most serious risks to physicians is that we lose touch with what we're actually in the business for, which is to provide care and an environment in which patients get well.

Some of this is being addressed in medical schools now. At the time of my second surgery, I had been working with a group at the University of New Mexico that was discussing how doctors might connect with patients on a deeper level and avoid the trap of seeing them only as an object in need of repair.

When the heart surgeon went through the formality—"Are there any questions?"—we asked a few superficial ones: "How long will this take?" That sort of thing. My brother, Andy, did most of the asking. I asked something about possible complications. The surgeon said it could be anything from stroke to heart attack to other less serious problems with the heart.

Then it was over.

"Is there anything else?" he said.

Silence.

"Then I'll see you tomorrow," he said.

He walked out and the doctors-in-training trailed after him.

What happened to the questions we had so carefully compiled? How could a roomful of medical professionals suddenly be struck dumb?

I don't know. I wish I did.

The intimidating factor of the surgeon's presence probably explains part of the questions' disappearance, but there is another component that carries more serious implications. I believe neither the surgeon nor any of the other doctors wanted to carry on a genuine discussion. No one said as much, but there was no need to, as their demeanor managed to get across the message without the formality of words. My sense was that they assumed whole chapters of my personal history and that while the surgeon continued to talk, there would be no two-way conversation going on. He said he had talked to my cardiologist and this is what we're going to do and that's the end of that.

And there *you* are, in the hospital bed, trying to process the information amid the fear and uncertainty and pain.

Until this moment, I was unsure of what to expect. I had never met this man. I had no feeling one way or the other except that he had been recommended by my cardiologist. When he finished speaking and said, "Are there any questions?," it sounded as rote as the speech itself, part of the requirements needed to touch the customary bases. I never had the feeling he was honestly inviting discussion.

I'm a busy man and I'm telling you what's going to happen. It's late, everybody's tired and we want to move on. I'll see you later. Any questions? None? Good. See you tomorrow.

I don't remember that he ever touched me to any degree except to shake my hand. I don't recall that he ever listened to my heart or lungs. He just walked in, said his lines and walked out. An odd vacuum lingered as he disappeared from the doorway. No one spoke for a moment. Until the surgeon arrived, the conversation had been light. In the wake of his exit a heavy silence descended.

What filled the vacuum was the awful reality. This was it. I could die tomorrow.

Everyone seemed wary. The silence in the room was eerie and unnatural. In retrospect, I look at it as a spiritual time. Perhaps there was no need to speak. It is possible the awkwardness of any conversation would have worked against us.

I did not sleep well that night. Typical for any hospital, I was awakened repeatedly throughout the night for one medical reason or another. The next morning, Beth came first, around six o'clock, then the others. Surgery was scheduled for eight. The previous evening's silence carried into the day.

CHAPTER ELEVEN

An emergency procedure bumped me from the 8 A.M. surgery. I did not leave my room until around one-thirty in the afternoon and I would not get into the operating room until around five o'clock. The delay was a repeat of what had happened in the first heart surgery in Albuquerque and was fairly typical. It was not uncommon for surgeries like mine to be justifiably delayed for more urgent procedures. What was not justifiable was the vacuum in which the hospital left my family.

Someone notified Beth when I had been taken into surgery. A second brief, sketchy report came around 6 P.M., an hour after surgery started. No one from the Medical Center would contact my family again until twelve-thirty the next morning.

Before the surgery I was going downhill quickly. I was tired and rundown and unable to recover strength no matter how long I rested. Just getting out of bed tired me. When the orderly came to get me, I was ready to go, yet the journey down the hallway was not without its own strangeness. It is an odd thing to be wheeled down a hallway on a hospital gurney. I had accompanied patients many times, but I always walked alongside the gurney then. Being flat on your back offers a much different perspective from that of the upright spectator at the gurney's side. Your world-view is from the waist up. People float by, as if they might be on one of those moving sidewalks in airports; glimpses of faces, lab coats, ties and surgical masks blur into a soft white focus periodically interrupted by a flash of color; Doppler effect conversations blend themselves into a meaningless buzz in your ears. You know your time is coming soon. For the most part you are optimistic, but in the back of your mind you wonder if these are the last things you will see in your life.

The orderly pushing me along the hospital corridors and into elevators was friendly and, as usual, I enjoyed the conversation with him. I have always liked talking to these guys whether I saw them when I worked as a doctor or surrendered to them as a patient. Whatever the conversation, there is something easy and relaxed about it.

The orderly left me in the surgery area and soon the anesthesiologist appeared.

"You aren't going to remember much after this," he said, preparing to inject something into me.

He was right. I did not remember much. But my family and friends were not so lucky. They remembered every minute, almost all of it in an information void that the Medical Center did little to fill.

A liaison whose apparent job was to deliver surgical updates to waiting families worked until around six o'clock, an hour after I arrived in the surgery area. The liaison delivered one report to Beth at quitting time, telling her the surgical team was getting ready to put me on by-pass. Then the liaison announced she was going home for the day. She said someone would "get in touch" with my family.

This happened nearly six hours later, and even then it was not by design.

By 11 P.M., my mother, my brother and Beth were exhausted. They decided to go back to the rooms at the Medical Center's Guest House because it was more comfortable there and they would have access to a telephone. The Guest House certainly held more appeal than the cavernous lobby in which they now were marooned.

The lobby was right off the main entrance to the hospital, the color scheme an unrelenting gray, the ceilings high, the walls a gray, polished granite. The carpeting was gray, two dull shades. A mauve stripe ran along the edge of it, an attempt to relieve the depressing effect of all that gray. Floor-to-ceiling windows rose on two sides. The seating and planters kept pace with the overall color scheme, the chairs uncomfortable gray squares. Presumably, the lobby seating is designed to discourage people from lying down and sleeping, although many people wait long hours. The end tables were upended gray laminate boxes, devoid of any reading material. It was as cheerful a place as any mid-to-late nineteenth-century mausoleum.

Further down the hall a gift shop offered a meager assortment of magazines and newspapers. Across from the gift shop was the admissions office, where we checked in the day before. The lobby hallway dead-ended at another hall, forming a T. Turn left and you run into a cafeteria the size of a bus station and just as impersonal. Turn right and you come upon a bank of elevators that take you up to the patient floors.

The space does not encourage people to hang around. But people do hang around, because they must. There is no place else for family members of patients undergoing surgery to wait. During the day, the lobby is crowded and the people awaiting news are on display to the constant stream of visitors and hospital staff entering and leaving the hospital. During my family's wait, they had asked everyone they could think to ask what the procedure was for notifying family members. They asked where they should wait after hours, they asked who would contact them with information about the progress of my surgery. No one seemed able to tell them. The nearby Guest House beckoned to them.

My brother, Andy, left word with a nurse in the ICU about where they were going. The ICU agreed to contact them when the unit was notified I was out of surgery. But this did not happen. Nonetheless, information has a way of flowing in unexpected ways and it would find its way to my family, and the way in which it did rocked the Medical Center's boat.

At the guest house, Beth called friends and family who awaited news in different parts of the country, giving them what little information she had. She talked to her mother and my father and said she would call when there was something to report. She called friends from the Presbyterian fellowship group. Before the night ended, the conversation with one, John Salazar, would have repercussions none of us could have anticipated.

John is a marvelous man, a superb dentist, a good friend and blessed with many strengths. But patience is not among them. He suffers delays poorly. Around 10 P.M., an hour before Beth returned to the guest house, John tired of waiting to hear news of my surgery and decided to call the Medical Center himself. He knew which unit I was to be admitted to after surgery and called the unit directly. A nurse answered.

John identified himself as Dr. Salazar from Albuquerque and said he was a personal friend of mine. He hoped that by doing so, they would give him a progress report on my status. They gave him considerably more than that.

The nurse said she didn't have any information yet. Before he could tell her it wasn't necessary to pursue the matter, she told him she would connect him to the operating room.

A few brief seconds passed and John found himself talking to an operating room nurse. He told her the same thing he told the nurse in the ICU. He was Dr. Salazar, a personal friend. He asked if she could give him a progress report. The operating room nurse told him to hold on a minute.

The next thing John knew, there was a man at the other end of the line who identified himself as my surgeon and addressed John as Dr. Salazar. The surgeon began to describe to John in detail the extensive necrosis and signs of infection discovered at the valve site. The aortic root was destroyed. He told John this discovery compelled him to modify the treatment plan and do a different procedure than was originally intended. He told John they had not been able to complete the procedure using a prosthetic valve.

By now, John realized who he was talking to and wanted only to find a graceful way out.

The surgeon explained the nature of the surgery, how the surgical team was forced to implant a homograft because of the infection present, that I was tolerating the procedure well and that they were close to completing the graft insertion.

When the surgeon finished, John said, "You have more important things to do right now, so I'll let you get back to Steve," and thanked him for his time.

Even now, when I think about this, it seems incredible that it could have happened.

Apparently, the ICU nurse who put John through to the operating room caught hell because when Beth called the ICU after arriving at the Guest House, a nurse supervisor read Beth the riot act. He accused her of conspiring to have John use his status as a "physician" to gain "inside information" and somehow undermine his authority as charge nurse.

Beth was stunned and confused. She tried to explain that she did not know anything about it, but the nurse would hear none of it. He continued his harangue even though she was apologizing profusely while not sure what it was she was supposed to be apologizing for. She knew only that this was not an auspicious beginning to my stay in the ICU.

The last thing the nurse said to her before slamming down the phone was, "Tell your friends not to call the ICU again."

She called John in Albuquerque. He told her what had happened. It may not have been official or authorized as far as the

Medical Center was concerned, but this is how my family came to find out what had transpired in surgery. Beth, an ICU nurse herself, had worked in hospitals for seventeen years and never experienced anything like it.

So when it became pointless to stay in the lobby, they went back to the Guest House. When she heard from no one by midnight, Beth called the ICU to see if I had been admitted, though she did so with some trepidation. She already had been yelled at by one ICU nurse earlier after John Salazar's call to the operating room, but she made the call anyway. There was nothing else to do. It was midnight. She could no longer stand the information vacuum. She had to call again. A different ICU nurse answered the phone.

"Oh, the surgeon has been trying to find you," the nurse said.

The arrangement my brother, Andy, made with the ICU nurses to call the Guest House when there was news of my surgery obviously had not been communicated. Beth was told to report to a small waiting area designated for families just off the entrance to the ICU unit. The nurse said I was on my way up from the operating room.

Beth and the others rushed to the waiting area—and waited more.

It was another cheerless place. Modular seating only slightly more comfortable than the gray boxes in the lobby spread around the perimeter of the room. A television mounted high on the wall blared a late night cable program.

The room contained a single occupant when my family arrived. Beth and Andy spent the next hour talking to him before I was brought upstairs. Their companion in the ICU waiting room was the father of the 2-year-old child who had bumped me on the surgery schedule. Before I was discharged, we would all develop a bond with this man. He had been living in the waiting room for days because he could not afford a hotel room. His child was born with a severe congenital heart defect and underwent three or four open-heart surgeries in her first year of life. She never lived outside a hospital. He said hospital bills had forced him to declare bankruptcy. The baby was at the Medical Center because the previous surgeries were not successful and she was failing. My heart surgeon had done a difficult and seldom performed operation in an attempt to save her.

About an hour after my family arrived back at the hospital, I was brought down the hallway outside the waiting room. I was accompanied by several staff members wheeling the gurney and life support equipment, a portable heart monitor, defibrillator, and an oxygen tank. A respiratory therapist stood at the head of the bed pumping the manual resuscitation bag that delivered every breath to me. Tubes attached to bottles and bags dangling from the stretcher snaked out from under the flannel blankets. From the waiting room, Beth, Andy and my mother were able to see me for a few brief moments before someone curtly told them that after I was settled in the unit my nurse would allow them to come into my cubicle.

About twenty minutes after I was admitted to the ICU, the surgeon appeared. He was still in his green scrubs. After completing my surgery, he had been in the unit working to stabilize the baby who was in extremely critical condition. Beth remembers him looking exhausted. He had been in surgery since eight o'clock the morning before. It was now one o'clock in the morning the next day and he was not yet finished. Beth wondered how many of his days were like that. Looking at the fatigued man standing before her, she thought that one had to pay a high price to be "God."

The surgeon sat with them in the waiting area and explained much the same thing he had told John Salazar earlier in the unexpected operating room phone call. He confirmed that the damage to my heart was much more serious than expected. He told them I had developed heart block which required a pacemaker after I was re-warmed. They also had to put me back on by-pass at one point in order to correct a bleeding problem.

During open heart surgery, the patient's body temperature is dropped to 17 degrees C or 62.6 F to reduce the body's energy requirements during surgery. The patient is re-warmed to bring the body temperature back to normal. Heart block occurs when electrical impulses that stimulate the heart to beat are blocked and the heart is not able to beat in the normal way. In more serious instances of heart block, the heart rate can drop to dangerously low levels, which requires intervention through temporary "pacing." Small pacemaker wires are positioned on the heart and lead out through the skin. They allow the use of a temporary pacemaker if needed, and it was in my case. The pacemaker delivered electrical impulses which stimulated my heart to beat.

Shortly after the surgeon left, a nurse came to the waiting room to tell them they would be allowed in to see me. The hallway outside the unit was dimly lit. The pneumatic double doors opened and they entered the self-contained world of the ICU.

The unit's dozen beds surrounded a large central area divided by the desk in the nurse's work station, which contained an impressive array of monitoring equipment and computers. My room was lighted by a harsh white fluorescent bulb in the panel above the bed. The top of the bed was elevated at a 45-degree angle with the side rails up.

The endotracheal tube in my mouth that brought air into my lungs was held in place by a wide strip of tape across my face. It was attached by a Y connector to the clear corrugated plastic tubes that stretched to the mechanical ventilator through which I breathed. The tubes were filled with heavy condensation from the warm vapor delivered by the humidifier.

My chest rose and fell in a regular rhythm, a cadence forced by the machinery and always accompanied by the characteristic hiss of the ventilator bellows. I was naked, covered to the waist by a thin white sheet. My chest was exposed. A bulky dressing covered my sternum. Thin, colored pacemaker wires peeked out from under the dressing. Round white electrodes held the monitor leads on my chest.

Four chest tubes, two on either side, protruded from wounds in my ribs and were secured to my skin with heavy silk stitches. They hung in loops winding down the bed into blood-filled Pleurovacs (water seal apparatus) bubbling on the floor.

A dressing on the right side of my neck covered the insertion site of the Swan-Ganz catheter. I had an arterial line in my left arm and multiple IV lines. About ten IV bags hanging from poles attached to infusion pumps surrounded my bed. They contained medications meant to keep my blood pressure and vital signs within a narrow range.

Beth could hear the beeps of the monitors, the wheeze of the respirator and shuffling sounds of the staff moving around in the nurses' station directly across from my cubicle. She could hear a patient being suctioned in the bed next to mine. A phone rang at the nurses' station.

She took in the indignity of it all—the noise, the smells, needles, tubes, catheters, wires, the harsh light, the ringing telephones, the unremitting pain I would experience upon awakening—all of it second nature to the busy medical professionals coming and going in the halls, a workplace white noise as they slipped in and out of my room to make routine checks on the status of that room's "customer."

I spent five days in the cardio-thoracic Intensive Care Unit, a unit that for all intents and purposes belonged to "God," my heart surgeon. It was a very busy place.

There was no bright light experience coming out of anesthesia this time, only snatches of consciousness in which the center of my universe seemed to be the breathing tube in my trachea.

I was off the ventilator quickly, always a big hurdle for cardiac surgery patients. Once you are off the ventilator and breathing on your own, then it is mostly monitoring vital signs and administering medications to keep them within a prescribed range.

As consciousness returned for longer periods, I became more aware of my environment, a complex of glassed-in individual cells. Each could be opened on two or three sides, allowing ICU staff to move freely from room to room. The main hallway was at the foot of my bed. The glass cell doors could be closed, but generally were left open, giving the patient a narrow, tunnel-like view of what's going on in what has now become his very small world.

I became more aware of pain. My chest felt compacted, as if someone had stitched it together too tightly. My skin had become a shirt three sizes too small; my breathing sounded shallow and felt restricted.

I was immobile, a medical Gulliver strapped down by lines and tubes and wires. All of it was familiar to me from the first heart surgery and already I was beginning to experience nervous anticipation. I knew that soon someone would come to remove the tubes and wires that protruded from my chest and I vividly remembered the feeling of being turned inside out. I had a terrible sense of being stuck, a prisoner who needed only to move an inch before pain reminded him that he had lost his freedom.

Throughout the day, if I tried to shift position to ease the pressure on my back, pain shot through my chest. Turning on my side was out of the question. I was strapped down, unable to control my bladder, unable to eat anything, thirsty and hoarse. The breathing tube damaged my vocal chords and I could speak only in a whisper. It would take almost a month to fully regain my normal voice. When I finally was given ice chips, I choked immediately and started coughing spasms that sent waves of pain rolling through my chest incision.

The medicines seemed endless. They came in tubes and paper cups, pumped into my veins, swallowed with sips of water until the nurses realized I could no longer swallow, a condition alleviated by medical technology's curtsy to mothers everywhere—the oral medicines were crushed into gobs of jelly and I was spoon fed.

With my view restricted to the narrow tunnel going out the door to the room, I watched the constant flow of activity. Noises came from every direction—patients next door, beepers going off, monitors tracking vital signs, alarms activating. Ventilators sounded tones that started out slowly, gently chirping, then growing louder until someone responded to the machines' insistent demands. In a little girl's glass cell not far from mine, one sounded like a child's melody, an ice cream truck making the rounds of a neighborhood. All day, all night, the ventilators sang their repetitive, maddening songs. In the background, babies and children cried, ICU staff hustled by the door, their conversations always at a normal workplace level and rarely in the hushed tones one might expect in such a place.

Nurses came and went, making their frequent checks. Seldom do I remember seeing the same nurse twice.

For years, there has been a serious shortage of nurses. Few hospitals have remained unaffected. Hardest hit are critical areas such as the intensive care units, cardiac units and emergency rooms, where special training is required. Hospitals often utilize contract nurses to fill the holes in their staffing schedules. The Medical Center was no exception; in fact I remember only two nurses who were permanent staff. I remember them being competent for the most part, but none connected to me on a human level, and if I had learned nothing else, I now knew the importance of caregivers making a connection to their patients.

The days were tolerable only because Beth or some other family member was there. The nights were anything but tolerable.

I would lie there listening to the noise of the ICU, uncomfortable and in pain, disconnected from any other reality.

The morning after surgery, Beth was allowed onto the unit after the shift report at 7 A.M. She was delighted to find me sitting up in the chair. I was much more alert than she expected. A young traveling nurse from New Zealand took care of me and when Beth volunteered to give me a bath, the nurse seemed relieved. The unit was full and she was assigned to two patients.

Beth filled a large basin with warm water and started washing my face. In a hoarse whisper, I told her about an unsettling incident that happened about an hour before she arrived.

I had asked for pain medication. While the nurse was giving the medication, I became queasy and lightheaded. I started to lose consciousness. It lasted only a few seconds according to the nurse, but when I came to, I felt terrible. I had a blinding headache. None of the nursing staff was able to explain the episode and what little discussion there was of it did not last long.

By nine o'clock, I was worn out. The nurse and Beth helped me back to bed. Beth asked the nurse for pain medication in the hope that I would be able to sleep for a little while. When the nurse returned with the medication, she went behind me to where a spaghetti tangle of IV lines were draped over the mattress and connected to the bank of IV bottles and infusion pumps encircling the head of the bed. Beth stood to my right, talking to me about trying to sleep. The head of my bed was elevated to a 45-degree angle.

For what happened next, I must rely on Beth's recall. Mine disappeared into a few moments of unconsciousness.

She said my eyes rolled back into my head and I slumped over. The color drained from my face.

She shouted my name. I didn't respond.

Beth reached over the side rails to support my body. She looked at the monitor and saw my blood pressure had bottomed out. Her first thought was cardiac arrest.

She slid the tips of her fingers from my Adam's apple to my left carotid artery to feel for a pulse. It was weak and thready.

The nurse flew around to the other side and wrestled with the bed controls to lower the head of the bed.

My eyes fluttered open. It took a few seconds to focus.

"What happened?" I whispered.

"I don't know," Beth said.

She took my face in her hands. Tears streamed down her cheeks.

In the seventeen years she worked in critical care, she had seen this scenario played out with ICU patients many times. Most didn't wake up. The code drill was so ingrained in her that she said she functioned like a robot when she saw my eyes disappearing into my head. With her training and experience, she had learned to disengage and perform her role automatically. When every second counts and concentration is focused on what has to be done, there is no room for emotion.

But when it is your husband, you don't disengage completely. Physically, Beth went through the drill, pulling me up in bed to feel for a pulse, checking the monitor for vital signs. But she screamed silently. I was dying and she knew it. It was as though two different people inhabited her body. The episode lasted probably no more than ten to fifteen seconds. She said it seemed an eternity.

In talking with the nurse after the dust settled, we pieced together what happened. The nurse said she had pushed my dose of morphine through one of the Swan ports. She never said which one, but there must have been Nipride in the line. Nipride is a powerful vasodilator that lowers blood pressure rapidly. It is not meant for direct IV injection.

When the nurse pushed the morphine, the Nipride in the tubing was propelled along ahead of it, essentially delivering a sudden infusion of the blood pressure medicine. In this case, the amount delivered would have been greater than what is normally given. Even small doses under these circumstances can have drastic effects and can cause severe hypotension (subnormal arterial blood pressure) and shock. This should never have been done. I had a peripheral IV line in my arm that could have and should have been used.

On the next shift, it happened again. Two nurses were splitting the shift. The nurse assigned to relieve the morning nurse used the wrong line for my pain medication. I lost consciousness again, as I had the first two times, but this time I came to in the "Trendelenburg" position, where the head of my bed was lowered and the foot pointed in the air. It is the position the bed is placed in when patients go into shock. I was happy to be alive, but nonetheless, losing consciousness three times in one day did nothing to instill confidence. Obviously, no one had reported what had happened during the nurses' shift changes.

In addition to the oral blood pressure medications I took, I had a drip going into the catheter in my neck that allowed for adjustments to keep my blood pressure within a desired range. For IV purposes, problems arose because my arms were useless; some of the medications I had been receiving were toxic and hard on my veins. Getting a needle into me became an exercise in futility. The veins would spasm and the blood wouldn't flow properly, resulting in painful searches for other veins. IV after IV was replaced. I soon became a pin cushion.

Probably the biggest insult came when an infectious disease doctor decided he wanted to give me a medication to prevent fungal infection, though there was nothing that indicated I had or was expected to get such an infection. He just wanted to "cover all the bases."

This medicine, amphotericin B, is known to be probably one of the most potent, toxic medicines they could give.

The warning label on the bottle is enough to give pause to the most stout-hearted: *Amphotericin B is frequently the only effec-*

tive treatment available for potentially life-threatening fungal disease. In each case, its possible life-saving benefit must be balanced against its untoward and dangerous side effects. Rapid infusion has been associated with hypotension, hypokalemia, arrhythmias and shock. Acute reactions include fever, shaking chills, anorexia, nausea, vomiting; headache and tachypnea are common. (It is toxic to the kidneys and liver.) *Overdose can result in cardio-respiratory arrest.*

A strict protocol is supposed to be observed in administering it. Because it interacts with almost every other medication, it has to be given by itself. They had pre-medicated me with acetaminophen and antihistamines (sometimes steroids are used) before giving it to prevent me from developing fevers. But even with all the precautions, the slow infusion is painful.

Throughout these preparations for administering the drug, I told the nurses the idea was not a good one, but it seemed an epidemic of deafness had swept over the ICU—and after all, who was I, a patient, to be offering opinions on such things?

During one Amphotericin infusion, my IV began "infiltrating," a situation in which the fluid no longer goes into the vein but into the tissue itself. I felt a painful burning that was considerably greater than the pain I had experienced with other infusions. The skin around the IV insertion site was red and puffy, evidence that the infusion wasn't going right. The ICU was busy and it took a while for the nurse to respond to my call light. When she entered the room she seemed harried and distracted.

She repositioned the IV catheter and the flow improved to her satisfaction, but she was not able to get a blood return from the IV catheter, which is proof that the IV line is not blocked. She resumed the infusion. I had the feeling she was not in the mood to start another IV on a difficult patient. Not surprisingly, the toxic drug did not go into the vein, but continued to be forced into the tissue. My arm continued to swell.

"It's not working," I said through gritted teeth the second time I called her back.

"I think it is," the nurse said.

As my arm ballooned, the pain intensified with each passing moment until the throbbing was almost unbearable. I ended up with a phlebitis and a severe local inflammatory reaction that took weeks to resolve.

After the third call, the nurse decided to try another site. Several unsuccessful attempts later, she got an IV started in my other arm. She demonstrated no remorse over creating a situation which should have been avoided by following established nursing procedure.

I doubt these incidents were written up by anyone on the three nursing shifts over which the events occurred. Beth was furious. I wanted only to survive. I didn't want to make anyone mad. I wanted only to get through it, though I was mad at myself for not saying anything. My arm was killing me. It was red and throbbing, swollen to twice its normal size and it would hurt for another two or three weeks.

Yet I felt powerless. If you are the patient, you tell yourself that you cannot afford to make anyone mad. You do not want medical staff to be in a position where they might act out of anger when providing—or not providing—your care. You are simply powerless.

After the first two days in the ICU, I was moved to another bed, one that would be "quieter." I do not know that it was any more quiet than any other bed, but I do know it was more humbling. Given everything that happened to that point, I found myself reflecting on what I had and what I might still lose.

I could barely see out the door, but there was enough open space to see an infant's father bustling around the ICU, doing everything he could to care for his critically ill baby. It was the man Beth and Andy had met in the family waiting area. We had heard more about the infant's condition from the nurses and the news was bad. The baby was going downhill. We watched the father and the grandmother go in and out of her room and Beth sometimes was able to talk with him in the ICU waiting area. On my last day in the ICU, the grandmother was interviewed on a television news broadcast, talking about the baby's plight. They were desperate for a heart donor for a transplant. And now the baby was crashing. I heard the nurses talking just outside my door. The baby wasn't going to make it.

I was almost 42 years old and at least had the opportunity to have a childhood, to know what it is like to fall in love, to marry, to have children and cherish them. I had been so fortunate. I had it pretty good, actually. I was in no position to complain about how cruel life had been to me or to be asking God how He could have let this happen to me. Despite everything, I was being given a chance to live life again, to see my kids, to be with my family. I had little to complain about.

CHAPTER TWELVE

Two days after New Year's, I was transferred from the ICU to the "floor." The move brought relief to all of us, but it was short-lived. Unaware that the bureaucratic wheels were grinding to create another unpleasant surprise, my family and I celebrated the prospect of more privacy for me and easier access for them that would come from my being out of the ICU.

The transfer order had been written early on a Saturday morning. As usual in hospitals, it often takes hours for a transfer to take place and it did in my case as well. I was not moved to the floor until early that afternoon. My cousin, David, had just arrived from the East Coast. My brother, Andy, and Beth wanted to take him to lunch. No one had eaten all day.

Before leaving, they made sure I was situated in the room and all was well. They were gone about an hour when Beth began to get anxious about returning. They decided to skip dessert, which was fortunate for me, because somewhere in the hospital a decision had been made, and it was not a good one.

The Medical Center was only minutes away from rolling me out the door to fend for myself. Shortly after Beth and the others left, a first-year resident came in my room with startling news. I was to be discharged from the hospital on the same day I was transferred from the ICU.

This preposterous notion came perilously close to fruition.

For a number of reasons, I was pretty well out of it and in no position to put up an argument. The effects of anesthesia for that length of surgery can linger for days or even a week before the patient regains full cognitive functioning. I was on multiple pain medications and having undergone a physical insult as extensive as open heart surgery, it was natural to be disoriented and unfocused. After we got back to Albuquerque, Beth said it took several weeks before she thought my mental acuity fully returned.

So when the resident came into my room, I was unable to speak for myself, not that he gave me much to go on anyway. He had no particulars, no specific information, no instructions, only a vague sense that somewhere, somehow, a decision had been made—I was to be discharged.

Someone brought a wheelchair and left it in the room. There would be no discussion or dallying. They meant to move me out. I sat in my hospital bed hoping and praying that Beth would return before I found myself on the sidewalk with my clothes bundled up in my lap. I could challenge nothing the young doctor said. Weak, sedated, and sick are not good starting points from which to begin an argument. When David, Andy and Beth returned to my room, my belongings were packed up, ready to be moved. I sat in a visitor's chair, the wheelchair nearby. It was obvious that the discharge was imminent.

"What's going on here?" Beth said.

As best I could, I told her.

Beth stormed out, headed for the nurses' station, which was just outside my room and close enough for all of us to overhear the conversation.

The nurse told Beth I was being discharged. The order had been written.

Beth pointed out that only an hour ago I was critical enough to be in the ICU. She asked the nurse if she thought I was well enough to go home. The nurse said she did not really think so, but there was nothing she could do about it. The order had been written. She had to follow it.

Beth asked who wrote the order.

The resident wrote it.

Beth asked the nurse to call the resident.

He's gone off duty.

Who was responsible for the resident?

The chief resident.

Beth asked the nurse to call the chief resident.

The chief resident was sleeping. The nurse could not disturb him.

Beth demanded that the nurse call the chief resident. The nurse refused.

By now, something was happening that hospitals everywhere dread: A scene was being made. People in the hallway began to notice. Hospitals dislike public "scenes." It makes the other patients nervous.

Beth asked about contacting the heart surgeon or the other attending surgeons.

Impossible, the nurse told her. They were *all* in surgery.

Beth asked the nurse to call one of the Clinical Nurse Specialists for the Cardio-thoracic Surgery team. They are the team members responsible for coordinating discharge planning and post-operative teaching. The nurse said she would do that.

Thirty minutes later, the Discharge Planner came to the room. She agreed that I was probably not ready to go home yet, but said her hands were tied, too. The order had been written.

She then said that a PICC line (Peripherally Inserted Central Catheter) would need to be done before I could be discharged and that it would take some time to arrange and perform. Perhaps by the time the PICC line procedure was completed the chief resident might be awake and available. Before she left to schedule the PICC insertion, we extracted a promise that she would watch for the chief resident and talk to him as soon as he was available.

After she left, we convened a strategy session. Having done everything we could from within the hospital, we decided to work from outside of it.

We called our HMO caseworker in Albuquerque. It was HMO policy to assign a caseworker to coordinate and follow complicated cases and in this instance, it was a godsend because we had a contact person to talk to when problems arose and she was skilled at untangling complicated red tape. Before we left Albuquerque, she gave us her home phone number and said if we needed to talk to her at any time to call her. We decided the time had come.

When told that the Medical Center was preparing to discharge me, she was first incredulous and then helpful. She said she had authorized a minimum of 10 hospital days and more if I needed it. She immediately started a round of telephone calls to forestall the discharge if possible.

In the meantime, the specially trained nurse came to insert the PICC line. Andy and Beth helped me back to bed. I was relieved to lie down. I was exhausted from sitting up in the chair. The nurse asked everyone to leave. Insertion of a PICC line is a sterile, minor surgical procedure that can be performed at the bedside. The nurse donned her sterile gown and mask. I was draped and the site was cleaned with an antiseptic. She had problems finding a site because of the phlebitis caused by the Amphotericin infiltration. It took almost an hour to do the procedure.

Around four o'clock, the chief resident came in. Animosity came with him.

It had been almost a week since I challenged him about signing the surgery consent form and clearly he had not forgotten it. He struck me as the kind of guy who did not make decisions on his own without checking with someone first, but he had gotten his hackles up when I refused to sign the consent form before speaking with the surgeon, and now I had the sense that payback time had arrived.

I doubt he made the decision to discharge me on his own, but it was clear he was not going to back down, regardless of its origin. He said he saw nothing inappropriate about it. Later that afternoon, though, the decision to discharge me was changed—but it took "God" to do it.

My heart surgeon came by on his rounds with his retinue of tired residents and medical students. Beth asked him if he really meant to send me home that day.

He looked around the room and said, "How many days has it been?"

"Four days. And he just left the ICU today," she said.

He counted on his fingers and said, "No, I think he should stay for three or four more days."

If looks could kill, the one on the chief resident's face would have put all of us in our graves at that moment. We had gone over his head and gotten an extension on the time. We had embarrassed him and he silently fumed, never saying a word, but without doubt furious.

Consider how frightening this situation would have been for an ICU patient who had no experience with the medical establishment. Consider how the family would have felt to leave for lunch only to come back and find their loved one had been discharged with no warning and no arrangements for continuing medical care. This "civilian" family, outsiders with no clue of the inner workings of a hospital, would have no earthly idea of what happened and would not know where to begin to get information. All they would know is that they now had a plethora of complex arrangements to make very quickly.

By the next day, I was feeling better. Getting out of the ICU and away from the constant monitoring of vital signs and assessments allowed me to get some much needed rest. I was also unnerved about the events of the "discharge" day and wanted to get out as soon as possible before anything else could happen.

I had the feeling, too, that once I left the ICU and was relegated to the "floor," things were going to get worse, that no one person would be in charge anymore. For all I knew, the person in charge now was a first-year resident.

I was discharged from the hospital the next day and stayed in California for three more days at the Medical Center Guest House. I was scheduled to see the surgeon one more time. It was important to me that I see him to ask questions, most notably the one concerning any more complications I might expect. I felt uncomfortable, run-down and I had trouble breathing. Each time we tried to take a short walk, I tired easily, usually not making it more than half a block before having to stop and rest. I didn't understand why, but I thought discussing this with the surgeon would provide some answers.

We convinced the surgery team that I needed to see a cardiologist and an appointment was made for the same day I was to see surgeon. I wanted the cardiologist involved in order to get some kind of consensus on my future care.

We then began a routine familiar to patients everywhere—postponements, cancellations, doctors unavailable, appointments rescheduled. The initial cardiologist became unavailable and another filled in, which was a blessing in disguise, as she was the first physician I had met at the Medical Center who seemed interested in me as more than a "valve."

On the day of the appointment with the heart surgeon, we were scheduled to see him in mid-afternoon. Early that morning we received a call that he would be busy at the scheduled appointment time and that we were drop whatever we were doing and immediately go to his office, only a block and a half away. Beth asked if I wanted to walk. I didn't. So we waited for the next shuttle. It took an almost an hour before it appeared.

At the hospital, we went to the cardio-thoracic division, where the surgeon had his office. A secretary said he was not in the building and that we would be seeing someone else. We had waited four days (the final day in the ICU and three more at the guest house) to see the surgeon who had operated on me. We made the appointment at his convenience, the day on which it would be best for him, not the other way around. All to no avail. We wound up speaking with an associate surgeon. I liked him. We both did. But it did little to alleviate a sense of abandonment.

I was history. I was gone.

The primary surgeon called me the next day, the morning we left for Albuquerque. He did not apologize and made no mention of the missed appointment. There was no sense of "Gee, I'm sorry we didn't really communicate about any post-operative complications you might expect."

I was a valve. A little more interesting than most, perhaps. But once the surgery was over, it seemed "God" had moved on to the next case.

On the other side of the coin was the cardiologist, who was everything a patient could ask for in a doctor. She asked questions: How are you doing? How is your family? What has this done to you?

I had a clear sense that she was not only a good physician but a caring one as well, someone who instinctively knew of the disruption to my life and my family. I wondered why in the world we had to wait until the very end of our stay at the Medical Center to meet a physician who seemed to genuinely care about the welfare of a patient.

I had asked earlier in my stay about seeing a cardiologist and I was told by a member of the cardio-thoracic surgery team that I would not be needing to do that, which I thought was at the very least interesting, if not irregular, given that I was facing cardiac surgery. I had seen an infectious disease specialist, a dermatologist, a gastrointestinal consulate. But no cardiologist. There is always rivalry among the specialties in a large teaching institution and sometimes these rivalries interfere with patient care. Usually, surgeons are at the top of the status pyramid and primary care at the bottom. Cardio-thoracic surgeons are elevated to a divine level. Mere cardiologists too often are regarded with condescension and considered unnecessary by the deities in the surgical setting.

The cardiologist examined me, spending a long time listening to my heart. She thought I had developed a pericarditis, which sometimes happens after a heart operation. It restricts movement of the heart and creates difficulties for the patient. She said it probably explained why I was having trouble breathing when I was flat on my back.

She suspected fluid had gathered around my lungs too, as a result of the surgery. When listening to my breathing, she heard rales (an abnormal sound) caused by fluid in the lungs.

"That's absolutely remarkable," I said to her. "Nobody ever told me any of this while I was in the hospital."

She did not respond to that, but she seemed bothered that no cardiologist had been involved until now. She did not seem pleased that I had been tossed out of the ICU with no one we could identify as having made the decision and that I was just now receiving information that would have answered several pressing questions days ago:

1. Why I was so tired.
2. Why I couldn't lie flat on my back.
3. Why I was having trouble breathing.

All of it would have relieved my mind considerably if I had known. Instead, I spent my time guessing, worried that the valve was leaking again or something had torn loose.

She encouraged me to call her at any time and I believe she meant it. I did not talk to her again, but if the need had been pressing, I would not have been reluctant to call, especially if I thought she could have helped in getting information from the Medical Center's bureaucracy, a daunting task.

With so many healthcare professionals among my family and friends, I had a formidable array of medical knowledge available to me. All waited for information from the Medical Center, most of which never came for reasons on which I can only speculate.

First, I had challenged the people who held the information. They weren't used to that. Many of these people were not out in practice, had not yet moved beyond their residency, and here came the Hsi family and friends, medical professionals but still outsiders not affiliated with the Medical Center. We could not possibly know as much as the insiders, and so the insiders probably asked themselves why they should give information to people who won't understand it or will misuse it in any event.

From my hospital bed, admittedly a poor vantage point, I was struck that no one ever came to my room to collect all of the relevant information on my case. The one person who should have known was a first-year resident, but he did not have the knowledge or experience to be talking to a roomful of physicians. We wanted more detailed medical information than he could provide. I do not believe the first-year resident ever comprehended all the ramifications of the procedure, either. He was in charge of writing all the daily orders for my case and taking care of day-to-day business and I'm not sure he ever knew much about what was going on.

His discharge summary sent to my cardiologist and rheumatologist in Albuquerque was woefully inadequate. It encompassed about a page and a third. My cardiologist showed it to me and said with a rueful laugh, "It doesn't give me any information. It's worthless."

To this day, I have no actual records other than the resident's summary. I have no complete operative notes, no complete history, no physical, no consultants' notes, not even a complete pathology report. A friend and fellow physician who works at the Medical Center was forced to undertake a cloak and dagger operation in order to get the most basic information about my record.

It was (and remains) unforgivable.

This was my medical record; this was the information that needed to go to my doctors in Albuquerque to guide therapy. We couldn't access it and I finally gave up trying. Each time we requested records, we were sent abbreviated forms and told there would be an additional charge if I wanted more. Even my physicians in Albuquerque could not gain access to my record at the Medical Center.

It took five months for my cousin, Dr. David Hsi, to get the Medical Center to release my pathology slides to the Harvard researcher who had offered to review them. This researcher is one of the most knowledgeable vascular pathologists in the world and the one who made my initial Takayasu's diagnosis. After finally receiving the slides, his interpretation differed significantly from Medical Center's. He reported no evidence of active Takayasu's in the slides he received, raising a question as to whether my disease was active during the last surgery. This could have had tremendous implications in terms of medication and even my concept of what was happening to me.

If so much of my therapy was guided by the readings on my pathology slides, it could have meant a very different approach. If my cousin had not persisted in obtaining the release of the slides, I would have continued to operate under the assumption as presented by Medical Center. Now I was faced with discordant interpretations.

I was angry. Relieved there was no active inflammatory process going on, I remained perplexed because I didn't know what it meant for the future and it still left the big question unanswered: How do I manage the disease now that I have this new interpretation?

It was frustrating that it took so long for the absence of Takayasu's to be found. I sent two releases; my cousin spoke with the pathology chief resident; I spoke with the pathology department; the attending rheumatologist spoke with the department and the assistant surgeon as well. It could have and should have taken only weeks for the pathology information to be provided. Instead, it took five months to get the slides to Harvard.

Why? I don't know. I never will know.

It is with no small irony that I look back at all of this, important and troubling as it may be, and watch it fade into the background of a few moments that would become the most significant spiritual event of my life.

CHAPTER THIRTEEN

It was the fourth night at the Guest House after my discharge from the hospital. My brother, Andy, who had returned home after my surgery, had flown back from Albuquerque to help Beth bring me home. He slept in an adjoining room. Beth and I slept in twin beds in the main bedroom.

I had been excited about returning to Albuquerque, but a lingering anxiousness blunted the anticipation. Thoughts of the future troubled me: What would my recovery be like this time? What could I reasonably expect for my future health? How would I be with my family this time? What would happen to my work? Would I ever return to my career or would I be disabled?

I could not sleep. I had trouble breathing. I was having a lot of chest and back pain. Moments came when I thought I would not live to see the morning.

I had resolved not to go back to the Medical Center. I didn't care what might happen because of it. I was not going back to the emergency room to have them poke and prod and then re-admit me. I could not take another minute of it. If I'm going to die, so be it, I told myself.

I was ready at that point. I was exhausted, emotionally and physically. I had no more strength. It was the second surgery in eighteen months. We had been through tremendous emotional upheaval yet again and I knew I could not go through it one more time. The prospect of death had loomed since entering the hospital in Albuquerque three weeks before. I was afraid and in pain. I had reached a point where I could not deal with it anymore. I told myself that death was preferable to the struggle. I gave up. I began a conversation with God.

Surely, You would not have worked such miracles in keeping me alive two times if you didn't have a reason for me to be alive. I know in my heart that You have a purpose for me to be here, and that I must figure out what it is.

My body grew heavy, yet I was relaxed. I couldn't feel the bed below me and I moved my arms to touch it.

I felt a presence. I had a tremendous sense that whatever might happen next, I was safe. I was loved.

A deep, male voice spoke: "In all things, seek love. Pursue love."

A feeling of great peace enveloped me and I felt secure in the knowledge that I was protected by His love. A sense of timelessness came to me, yet I was acutely aware of everything I was experiencing—the surroundings of my room, my body and this extraordinary message from God.

I felt a release from my suffering. God was saying that love would be my way in this world. I felt (and still do feel) confused, not knowing what it all meant. God was saying that I was forgiven for all my worries and doubts and that I should trust that in striving for love, I will find purpose and direction.

Through it all, there was a sense of forgiveness for my smallness and failures. Fear and anxiety slipped away from me.

I have no idea how long it went on. It may have been seconds, it may have been minutes.

I said to God: *I will trust in You. Now I will take a medicine in order to go to sleep. If You want me to leave this Earth, then I know I will go to a peaceful, beautiful place. But somehow I believe You have reason for me to continue here in this world. If this is true, I will sleep and upon awakening I will not be short of breath and I will have less pain.*

All through my illness Beth and I had prayed. Sometimes alone, sometimes together, we always believed that He heard and that somehow He would answer. I took the sleeping medication and lay back in the bed.

At some point, Beth woke up. She went to the sink, got something to drink and came to me and knelt at the edge of the bed, as if she knew I were awake. She rubbed my forehead and ran her fingers through my hair.

"Are you okay?" she said. "I had this feeling that something was happening to you."

I told her what happened.

Eventually, I did fall asleep and when I woke in the morning, I was not short of breath and I was in less pain. Even now I think back and wonder if it really did happen. Then I quickly dismiss doubt. I have rolled the memory over in my mind countless times. I have wondered if I was hallucinating. Where did it come from? Was it the voice of God? Was it my own inner voice?

I believed then and I believe now that it was God. I came to realize that the question of its origin was unimportant. What was important was the message that changed my life.

In all things, seek love. Pursue love.

I had never thought in those terms. As everyone does sooner or later, I had repeated the clichés about all of us having a purpose in life and that sort of thing, but I never thought that the goal, the whole purpose of my life, and perhaps everyone's life, is to pursue love. Those moments left me with a strong sense that I needed to stand back and hear the messages coming from within myself. I could now let go of things that used to irritate and frustrate me. I no longer feared anything. I had believed all along that God was there for us. Now I knew it for a certainty.

In the days to come this absence of fear would change the way I approached my patients and my friends. In the past, where I had been guarded and protective of myself, I could not imagine opening up to people in the way I did after that night at the Medical Center Guest House. I found myself looking beneath the surface in conversations with patients and friends. I sought more depth in all of these relationships.

I began feeling people out for what was most important to them. I wanted to know how they felt about their families and themselves. With my own fear dissolved, I more easily understood that it is the fear of rejection and not being loved that prevented many people from reaching out to one another and running the risk of revealing themselves. I had always prided myself on being a good listener, but I now listened more for what was unsaid in conversations. I was not afraid to voice those things often left unspoken.

At first I thought my interest in deeper, more revealing matters would appear threatening; instead, I found people were relieved to talk about the things that preyed on their minds but that they kept hidden away.

I never had much patience for superficial conversation (and even less for superficial people), but I found myself being more forgiving, and in so doing, more easily forgave myself for perceived flaws that in my perfectionist past would have caused anger and self-doubt. I felt secure in God's love. It gave me the freedom to let go and extend myself to others. When you are sure of God's love, you are not afraid of risk.

I am not nominating myself for sainthood. Far from it. But that night changed me. I would still be plagued by moments of uncertainty, but each time I overcame them, I became more resolved to seek love in all things.

CHAPTER FOURTEEN

Home startled me. We live in an old adobe house in Albuquerque's North Valley, an area of small urban neighborhoods and sprawling semi-rural estates, all of it close by the banks of the Rio Grande. The house stood vacant and was in foreclosure when we bought it on the county courthouse steps. Vandals had trashed it and we worked hard to restore it. Like all New Mexico adobes, it has no sharp angles. Each imperfect mud brick was formed, turned and laid by hand. Adobe rounds off the edges where thick interior walls meet. With no sharp angles, the house creates an inviting space that envelops you as soon as you walk in. Older adobes seem softer still, as if the mud bricks had evolved into something almost maternal, strong enough to provide shelter, gentle enough to provide comfort. The sunlight streaming into our living room seemed delicate. It washed the plaster walls with a golden tint and warmed the brick floors. The faint scent of piñon wood mingled with the sweetness of rosemary brought in for the winter.

My memory was still of the hospital—the smell of alcohol, cleaning agents, urine, feces.

I stopped inside the French doors that led to our dining room and looked across the living room. The kiva fireplace in the corner still held the ashes of a recent fire. Beth's touch was everywhere—Talavera pottery, New Mexican tinwork, Mexican masks, *retablos, bultos,* a painted processional cross on a stave, a brightly painted Oaxacan lizard slithering across a wall near the fireplace,

Day of the Dead sugar skulls from Mexico, *Doña Sebastiana's Carreta de los Muertes.*

I took it in with a sense of wonder. It was as if I had forgotten it all.

The silence of the house felt almost oppressive. I had become accustomed to the noise of alarms and televisions left on and people walking back and forth through the halls and continual interruptions. It took a few moments to reacquaint myself with where I lived.

I looked out in the back yard, where Beth's rose garden would bloom in a few short weeks. I turned to the southern windows, where the crab apple tree waited to shade the adobe-walled courtyard and send blizzards of pink blossoms showering down on the small patch of grass.

I felt as if I had slipped into the cushions of an old, favorite chair.

I had learned about the limitations of hospitalization; I had learned that even under good care and the best outcome, the separation from one's spiritual ground can deplete the will to heal. I learned how bad care could lead to the desperation to refuse treatment or even leave before discharge.

Now I was home. This is where I would heal.

I had tolerated the plane ride home fairly well and our reception committee—friends and my parents—were welcome faces. When I stepped outside the airport, New Mexico's light reminded me again of why painters and photographers find it irresistible. I was back in the high desert, the air clear and dry, the colors crisp and bold.

I was overjoyed to see the boys when they came home from school later that afternoon, but their greeting was reserved and quiet. They didn't rush up and give big hugs. David is naturally quiet and Andy didn't talk much about how difficult our lives had been, though I'm certain he feels the stress. There was a sense that things were better and yet I couldn't rid myself of the toll my sickness had taken on them. Each time I came back from a surgery or other medical procedure, it was difficult for me to focus on their needs and it was hard on them. They didn't get the attention they needed and deserved. I resolved to talk to them about it and to ask how it affected them. More than anything, I needed to know what I could do to help them.

I came home in the first week of January on a day that was sunny and warm in the morning but blustery and cold by late afternoon, a weather change that presented me with medical bookends—after the first surgery I was heat intolerant; now I could not stand the cold.

Our bedroom, an unsolved heating and cooling mystery, was the hottest room in the summer and the coldest in the winter. We had spent a small fortune having the heating and cooling systems repaired and improved but to no avail. Two blankets, two comforters, and still I shivered.

After a few days, I moved into a warmer guest room. Regardless of the medical explanation (my guess was inflammation, loss of muscle tissue and lowered metabolism), it could be 70 degrees in the house and I would wear a down jacket all day. The cold forced me to park in front of the fireplace in the living room. Beth built a fire every morning before she left for work and she would have the boys bring in a supply of wood so all I had to do was toss in a log when needed. I sat in the same favorite chair, feet propped up, reading and writing materials and a telephone nearby. I didn't leave the chair for a hours at a time.

Saturday
February 1, 1997
   My friends gave me a diary and pen and told me that I am getting a clear message to write about my experiences. It may take me awhile to get the hang of this. I'm still trying to figure out how to use this pen.

It is the first day of my 43rd year. Last night I celebrated my birthday with Beth and friends. Over the past years, there has been a shift in the relationships within the fellowship group. We have gone from being friends and having fun together to being a true family in which we have all developed deep love and caring for one another. Throughout my illness, these people have been there for me completely. They have given me strength during my hours of weakness. Such giving overwhelms me. It has taught me important lessons about sharing. It makes me feel small and inadequate.

The ice and snow retreated in February. Beth and I took long walks along the Rio Grande *bosque*. The Spanish word means "forest," and in the Rio Grande's case, it means a tangle of cottonwoods, Russian olives, salt cedars and twice a year, a sky filled with migratory Sandhill cranes.

The first day we walked, the ground was wet and firm. Horses had begun to leave tracks in spots, loosening the sandy soil and making walking difficult, but it did nothing to lessen the enjoyment. It was during these walks that Beth and I always made plans for the coming year. The *bosque* was our brainstorming place. This first walk after surgery brought talk of routine, and I savored it—building a fence, putting in raised garden beds, planting, painting. What a joy it was to speak of the ordinary tasks of a household.

But I could not escape medical realities. I had a peripheral IV through which I received antibiotics for about six weeks. Twice a day, ninety minutes each time, I would hook up and administer the medications. I found myself more impatient with the process this second time around. I was antsy. I wanted to get everything over as soon as possible. My mind would not allow me to be still. I could not stay focused on one activity for very long and I'd jump from one to another. It made the days seem very long. I tried to fill out paperwork—disability insurance companies, trying to pry information from the Medical Center bureaucracy. Time dragged. I could not do much. I spent a lot of time watching the clock, waiting for my wife and children to come home.

Sunday
February 2, 1997

Andy is now 11 and David, 8. I enjoy being with them. They are both growing up rapidly and becoming more independent. It is hard to believe how quickly time passes, how our babies have disappeared to be replaced by these fine boys. I'm grateful that we have this time together. Physically, I'm less able to do things, although I am now more mentally alert. But I find that I am more restless, wanting to do more. I try to meditate, but it is frustrating. I cannot settle my mind. I find I am happiest when my family is home.

I spent more time with my parents, which creates its own peculiar set of complexities, especially for a middle-aged man who prides himself on independence and self-reliance. With Beth back at work, my father helped me get the kids to school. My mother came by every day to fix a hot lunch and the habit gave us a lot of time together we otherwise wouldn't have had. Long talks made me realize I had become so focused on my personal needs that I hadn't realized how my illness had affected her. I think those hot lunches made her feel good that she finally could do something to help a son who was more apt to fix his own lunch than ask for help. Yet it was discomfiting to be driven around town by your parents and to have your mother stop by to feed you. Odd feelings of dependency nagged at me. In the end, though, my illness probably allowed us to enjoy being together in ways that we couldn't when we were younger.

Then there were the cats—Domino, Rags and Yo-Yo. Much has been written about the healing benefits animals have on the sick. Many hospitals have programs in which animals are brought in to visit patients. If our cats are representative, I am a believer. They seemed to know when something was wrong. They went everywhere I went. When I stopped, they stopped. When I moved, they moved. They had a way of bringing change to an otherwise dreary day. No matter how bad you might feel or how emotionally down you might be, a cat inexplicably jumping through a doorway suddenly makes things a little better.

Thursday
February 6, 1997

I awoke very early with a severe headache. Just about as far back as I can recall, even to first grade, I have had severe, pounding headaches that would build in intensity. They were clearly migraines, although they weren't ever given a name until I was in medical school and received treatment at the student medical center.

It's often baffling to me when I think back on this. I wonder how many people suffer from recurrent illness to which they have grown accustomed, never thinking, or worse, fearful, to seek medical advice. People who suffer from recurrent and chronic disease don't know what it is like to be normal or to feel good.

I took some medicine for my headache, had a small breakfast and read the paper. Gradually, the pain ebbed. I found myself feeling very clear and energetic for the first time in months. I recall having a few days last year in which I felt good. My mind was clear, my body relaxed. I felt euphoric. Today I am delighting in this good energy. I am hopeful that this is what "normal" is and that I can feel normal all the time.

As the weeks passed, there wasn't much self-pity. If anything, I was just grateful to be alive and home. Sitting in the chair before the fireplace, I looked back on the surgeries and it all seemed a dream, as if none of it happened.

Healing's complexities asserted themselves. Twice now death had come to my door and backed away. Healing, especially after a life-threatening crisis, is more than simply dealing with the physical aspect of trying to get something fixed and getting on with it. It deals with the whole meaning of life and what happens at death or when one is dying. It deals with spirituality, the psychological turmoil, the relationships you have with friends and family.

It involves community, too, and once again, I was astounded how friends had come together on my behalf. It was sometimes hard to stand by and watch. Being physically impaired requires a very different attitude. There is often a feeling of weakness and, yes, a sense of shame in not being able to do the things that once came so easily.

Each time these people came to my home, I was reminded that we are mistaken if we think we can send someone out to deal with the difficult job of healing and expect the sick person to do well when there is no community to support him. The importance of community cannot be properly measured. Its value is too great.

Sunday
February 9, 1997

Friends push "alternative" therapies. I struggle with these suggestions and I often am distressed at the number of people who go to them. So often "alternative" medicine is discussed as a backlash to Western medicine's inability to "cure" someone's problem. Certainly conventional medicine has its drawbacks— over-reliance on medication, poor communication and lack of caring.

Yet this society has in many respects created a situation in which medical doctors are held to defined standards of practice that disallow alternatives. Patients too often expect quick cures and medications for diseases or problems that would be best

treated through lifestyle changes and alterations in one's thinking.
But people don't want to change. They want an easy remedy.

It is hard not to become cynical and disillusioned as a physi-
cian. Medical doctors are expected to have all the answers and
cures while being controlled about our way of practice.

Long hours in front of the fireplace often turned to reliving
the ICU experience at the Medical Center. I involuntarily re-
played the days and nights until the memory almost became a
Post-Traumatic Stress Disorder experience. Like an old rock and
roll tune that pops into your mind unbidden, the song of the
ICU ventilators played over and over. I found myself humming
and whistling it, the melody almost a musical score, an intro-
duction to the ICU "videotape" that started up again in my
memory. The ventilator was at first like a Peruvian whistle, slow
in the early notes, then speeding up. Over and over. Fifty and
sixty times a day. It became like a hymn to me, something
learned forever as a child after hearing it sung repeatedly in
Sunday school classes.

Other sounds returned, some in harmony with the ventilator's flute, some discordant: the constant sucking sound of the
respirator; beepers going off; telephones ringing; a woman
speaking to her infant in Japanese; residents yelling down
the hallway.

Sometimes I wanted to rise from my ICU bed and shout:
"Don't you people know? Don't you care that there are people in
here dying? Doesn't it matter to you that there are families watching their loved ones die? And you're yelling jokes across the room?
Don't you care?"

When the anger subsided, memory brought humility and
regret. When I was a resident, my colleagues and I did the same
thing. We stood around in the ICUs with the attending physician
and told jokes, oblivious to the patients.

If you are a patient, you never really know what any cluster of medical staff is talking about. If they are laughing outside your door, you become a little anxious and wonder if they're making jokes about you. It's like those social situations in which you walk up on a group of people who are talking and when you arrive, the conversation stops. The young doctors will be outside your room, talking and joking, and when they come in your room, the conversation stops, and you are left with the feeling that you have intruded on something private. It's almost embarrassing.

Wednesday
February 12, 1997
Had a doctor's visit. My rheumatologist, Dr. Eddie Benge, was the first doctor to notice my new heart murmur. He had decided I should restart methotrexate. I have mixed feelings about this. Dutifully, I took my first dose of 5mg with folic acid and as before I developed mild nausea and flu-like symptoms. Inwardly, I often revolt against medications. I worry about what they are doing to me even while I realize there are often good reasons to take them.

My cardiologist, Dr. Paul Cochran, wanted to take things slowly and said I shouldn't think about returning to work for six to eight weeks. The workaholic doctor I had been clashed with the patient I had become and who now recognized the importance of balancing work and health and family. It seemed at times the internal argument would go on forever. My friend, John Salazar and I were talking about the pressures society at large and the medical profession in particular put on people to identify themselves with their ability to work.

"Let them go through what you have gone through and see how they feel about returning to work," he said.

Our society values work and earning money so highly that we use these as markers for well-being and have come to expect that returning to work should happen soon after one has improved from a serious illness. The medical community is often the worst offender in this. Doctors are not open to discussing it. At the time, I didn't feel I was ready to handle patient care and while that assessment may have been both physically and psychologically accurate, I felt guilt nonetheless.

I settled into a pattern of rest and discovery. I found new delight in routine chores, the most enjoyable was driving the boys to school. Andy had reached an age where his conversation flowed in a disconnected stream of consciousness that flooded its banks. After dropping Andy off at his school, there was such a quietness in the car that it was like stepping outside after a loud concert.

Once Andy was at school, David and I had an hour before the start of his school day and we often spent it at McDonald's, always David's idea of fine dining. David sat across from me, eating his Egg McMuffins and drinking his orange juice, answering my questions with one or two words, my quiet son, who hums when he is content or busy working on a project.

On these mornings at McDonald's, we were surrounded by older men, retirees who made this their gathering spot. I liked the atmosphere. Breakfast smells wafted through the air, papers rustled as the men read their newspapers, lids snapped off plastic cups, voices low, as if there might be an unwritten code of ethics prohibiting loud noises. I caught pieces of conversation. They often centered around illness and dying.

Weeks passed and my recovery went well. Heart tests looked good. Beth and I went to parent-teacher conferences. We spent a weekend with friends, cross-country skiing at their Angel Fire cabin.

Small victories came. I fixed a flat tire and it felt good to do it. Beth worried I was pushing things. Her concern irritated me. It shouldn't have.

I found that I often was happiest when doing small tasks using my hands. I got into a "flow" mentality and time disappeared.

Beth and I traveled to Phoenix for a drug company conference. I made the trip with no trouble, but found myself uncomfortable with the physicians working for the drug company. Listening to them make their presentations, I sensed in them the old attitude of superiority and greater knowledge. Much of it probably is unintentional and possibly even protective as they have allowed their "professionalism" to dictate their demeanor to the world. I disliked the way they distanced themselves, separated themselves from the world. I know this prevents them from learning about the people for whom they "care." It saddens me.

Tuesday
April 22, 1997
I returned to work yesterday. It was better than I imagined it would be.

CHAPTER FIFTEEN

My patients became my healers. I had received many cards and letters from them. They notified their churches—Baptist, Catholic, Methodist, synagogues, my own Presbyterian church. They put me on prayer lists. Here were people I had seen only a few times in most cases and they had opened their hearts to me. It humbled me and reminded me again of the power of community. Knowing so many people cared so much lifted my spirits. That knowledge alone makes you want to recover. They had been supportive of us through the first surgery and I didn't think they would (or could) be there as much the second time. If anything, the opposite was true. They were there for us even more.

It was a great relief to be taken in by that community. People took my vulnerability and turned it around to provide me with strength. I had become almost like an open book in some way. My life was exposed to my patients and whatever guard or shield that kept me from being open to them in the past suddenly was gone. I am certain that a large part of that openness came from an acknowledgment of my own helplessness in the situation.

I was not greater or lesser than anything. I was part of the community. I was experiencing the process of life and death and even though I was vulnerable, I was free. I didn't need to keep my guard up.

Physicians erect great barriers to appear less vulnerable and it prevents us from reaching our own spiritual selves. The idea of humanity is very much tied in with vulnerability. To be truly human, to be part of the community, we have to recognize our helplessness in a lot of things and our dependence on other things and other people. Being reminded of that allowed me to begin a conversation with my patients. I talked more easily with them about my experiences and I believe it allowed me to create a stronger bond with them, though in truth they were the ones who often turned the tables first.

As I enter the examination room now, before I have a chance to say a word, the patient will say, "Well, how are *you* doing?" And I'll say I'm doing fine, but we're really here to talk about you, at which point the patient will deliver a gentle lecture about how I shouldn't "overdo" it.

They have allowed me to feel a sense of kinship with them. They have taught me that the ostensible reason for which they have come to me may be only the superficial one, that something more important lies beneath the surface and the only way I will discover it is to be open with them. Two heart surgeries have closed the distance between us.

Thursday
April 24, 1997

I completed my first week of part-time work. I did feel tired after just half a day. I saw many old patients and friends. It felt like I had never left. I had a few difficult patients. Both have diabetes and vascular diseases, yet I feel neither is doing much about it. I'm realizing how much people take for granted in their health.

I've had a headache all day, which is most likely due to the methotrexate.

Thursday
May 1, 1997

I finished the last shade structure today for the back yard patio. I still plan on building a front door entrance in the near future.

I lowered my dose of methotrexate to 5mg to see if my headaches decrease. I had one last night and again upon rising. It's difficult to know for sure, but the timing would suggest methotrexate.

Monday
May 5, 1997
Cinco de Mayo

David is interviewing Beth for his homework project. They're lying on our big bed looking at her old photo album. Beth is telling David about growing up in Indiana. David laughs at her crazy exploits riding piglets and playing in the barn. I wonder if it all sounds too fantastic to him to imagine life without television, computers and fax machines. I wonder what fantastic tales his children will hear.

Saturday
May 31, 1997

I have been disappointed at the Spiritualness in Health Care meeting this week. Once again the attendees spoke clinically and more distantly. I was saddened that the questions of our own personal spirituality were avoided. I'm worried that as clinicians we will lose the focus of trying to provide support and understanding and instead will lose ourselves in "third-person" dialogue. My question is why we find it so difficult as physicians to approach our own injuries and shortcomings. Why can't we let our guard down? Is it because we have become so good at concealing or burying our sensitivities that we cannot find them within ourselves?

As I write this I am suddenly aware that there were no nurses at this meeting. They often are more able to express and share their feelings.

Prayer is so hard to understand. I am convinced it aided my recovery. But I cannot explain it. There is no objective sense of it. There is only the certainty in my mind that it was effective. To raise such a question in a group of physicians indeed felt like exploring unknown territory.

Ask patients and most say they believe in a spiritual life; ask doctors and many of them are unwilling to admit it or recognize it in their patients. They simply do not want to talk about it. But if we don't acknowledge a patient's spirituality, in a sense we're negating what they are trying to convey to us. We deny what they clearly tell us.

It is like closing a door on them, and as the door shuts, we say to them, "This can't be. This is not true."

I felt that many times in the hospital.

I was one of several physicians and nurses who formed a study group to examine the role of faith in healing after we attended a conference—"Spirituality in Health Care"—held in Albuquerque in late February. I was encouraged by the attendance at the conference, though I could not help but notice the dearth of private practice physicians. The majority of people at the conference came from the University of New Mexico, especially from the family practice program. Still, the conference was exciting and the speakers—Dr. Dean Ornish, Dr. Herbert Benson, Dr. Larry Dossey—all lived up to their billing.

Soon after the conference, we began to meet on Thursday nights to discuss how spiritual matters might be woven into the medical school curriculum and to explore our personal feelings about spirituality and how we could apply them in our own medical practices.

But we soon slipped into the dispassionate third person, the comfortable place in the distance physicians are trained to seek and embrace. It is easier there. We didn't talk about personal matters but more about how we taught spirituality to young people and why doctors are the way they are and what's happening to our healthcare system and that sort of thing.

In other words, we quickly found the more comfortable—and wrong—track.

I asked why doctors are afraid and almost embarrassed to talk about spiritual matters. What was it about their spirituality that created the barrier? Why do we erect such a barrier?

I got no answer. The subject was shifted to something else, though it was the reason we had gathered, the guiding principle of the Thursday night meetings. It seemed we did not know how to put that principle into practice. Each time I talked about personal spiritual beliefs, I sensed they were thinking—*That's a nice story. Now let's move on.*

I came home from these meetings with doubt. I thought back to the night at the Medical Center's Guest House and wondered if my divine encounter had happened or if I had imagined it and only spun it from a whole cloth of pain and fear. The moments of doubt were not news to me. I'd had them before and always came back to the same place: No, I didn't imagine it. It happened.

I said to the group, "You can't objectify it. You have to take this leap of faith. You have to believe it happened or you have to say it didn't and throw it all away."

I still believe medicine and spirituality can be brought together to benefit the patient, but to do it, the physician must honestly admit what he doesn't know; he must put aside prejudice and acknowledge that much of healing is a mystery. Of course, this would require some degree of humility, a commodity often in short supply in the medical profession.

It took scientists centuries to throw off the restrictive yoke imposed by religion. It remains a struggle to this day. Many scientists view a marriage between the spiritual and medicine as regression. This is hammered into us early in our training. The pursuit of knowledge, logic and reason is the ultimate goal. Think with your brain, not with your heart.

Saturday
May 21, 1997

Yesterday, I met a man who was picking up his granddaughter from our friend Brenda Kilcup's house. His daughter (the girl's mother) committed suicide about a year and a half ago. Since the birth father was divorced, he has been distant from the family and the grandparents assumed custodial rights of the girl. He told me a story of when he was severely ill and in the ICU and on life support for about three weeks. He came very close to dying.

Then he volunteered this: He said a "Godly" voice came to him and said, "Paul, you need to stay alive. It is not time for you to die now."

He said the voice was clear as could be. Shortly after that, his wife became seriously ill, his daughter committed suicide, and he was needed. I felt a calmness and a closeness to him. I told him my own story and I believe we shared a strong sense of understanding. It made me feel better at a time when I was beginning to think that the rest of the world would not believe my own hearing of God's voice.

Sometimes I wonder that if you are open to them, these messages are so clear that they just hit you in the face. I had just gone to the Thursday night meeting and I was having feelings of self-doubt. All of sudden He reaffirmed everything.

As we headed into summer, the days became a mixture of routine and quiet worry. The prosaic moments of everyday life seemed blessings to me—children's music recitals, clinic work, household chores, a bike ride through Chaco Canyon, camping at Ghost Ranch in northern New Mexico, a trip to Disney World in Florida.

Juxtaposed to the routine were the changes illness had brought—my headaches, which sometimes lasted for days, regardless of how I adjusted the methotrexate; my unnatural worry about something as mundane as catching a cold, because no matter how inconsequential a sniffle might be, each change brings a new worry that the cause lies somewhere in my heart; my apprehension about being too hard on the boys because time had become so important to me, compressed if not distorted, and I was unsure of how much I might have left. I was continually warring against the constant urge to push them, and often failing. It was especially so with Andy, the oldest.

The first week of June began a round of anniversaries, beginning with the severe chest pain two years ago that began this process of self-discovery. Two weeks later, another milestone—my first surgery, the transition from physician to patient. Then the Fourth of July, the day I came home from my first surgery.

Saturday
July 5, 1997

I slept fitfully. I'm not sure why I awaken so often. I manage to fall back asleep eventually, but not for long. I felt a deep sense of despair. I had a strange sense that my life was coming to an end and that I needed to prepare myself.

I awoke this morning from a dream, a nightmare about being a medical student at the Medical Center. I was living in a dormitory, but somehow had completely lost my direction. I had missed several lectures and was sorely behind in my course work. I didn't even know when or where my classes were held. I was very afraid of failure. I felt isolated and alone.

I am not sure what this means, except somehow I am feeling trapped with no way out.

Thursday
July 10, 1997

The boys and I went to John Salazar's dental offices today. I had my teeth cleaned. This was the first time I have had to take prophylactic antibiotics for any procedure. The thought of endocarditis is frightening, so I have no reservations about doing it. Who knows? Maybe it will clear up my sinuses.

New Mexico's "monsoon" season has begun. The skies darken as the clouds thunder in every afternoon, but so far there has been only much sound and fury and little in the way of rain.

Beth's sister arrives tomorrow for a week.

Thursday
July 17, 1997

Terrifying! Awakening early Sunday morning feeling restless and panicky but not sure why. Try to go back to sleep but cannot stop. Then aware that I have no control of my arms and legs. I try to get up, but I can't get my feet to cooperate. I realize something is terribly wrong and I must awaken Beth. I toss and turn trying to reach her.

Finally, she asks, "What's wrong?"

At first, she thinks I'm dreaming. Later she tells me I said clearly, "Where is the boomerang?"

"I CAN'T TALK!"

The words are garbled. She doesn't understand.

Beth quickly rolls out of bed and turns on the light. My thinking seems clear, but I cannot control my speech.

"S-T-R-O-O-O-K-E!" I try to tell her.

CHAPTER SIXTEEN

Beth turns on the bedroom light. She sees the right side of my face drooping. I am thrashing violently, tangled in the sheets and blankets. She asks if I can understand her. I am able to nod my head. She asks what is happening. I manage the word again.

"SSS-T-R-OOOOKE!"

Beth races out of the bedroom to wake up her sister, Cris, who was visiting and who is a nurse, too. Beth then dials 911. I can hear her speaking clearly.

"He's had a stroke, I think. No, he doesn't have any chest pain. He can't talk or swallow. No, he is breathing okay. He can't walk."

I try to talk. The words disintegrate in my throat.

I struggle to sit up, but I can't do it. Beth tries to get me to lie quietly. I can't do that, either.

She kneels on the floor next to the bed, her face close to mine.

"I know you're frightened," she says. "I won't leave you. I'm right here. I'll stay with you."

I begin to cry.

It seems only minutes before I see the flashing lights pull into our driveway. Cris opens the bedroom doors onto the courtyard and calls to the paramedics. Then she runs down the hall to close the boys' bedroom doors.

A paramedic talks to Beth. His partner slaps a blood pressure cuff on my arm. He calls out numbers. The paramedic talking to Beth scribbles them on the palm of his hand with a ball point pen.

I toss about on the bed and groan. Beth holds me, crying, trying to remember the answers to questions the paramedics ask.

"H-E-E-L-L-P M-E-E!" I repeat again and again.

No one hears me. The words stay trapped inside me, prisoners of my body, just as I am. They race from my mind fully formed and whole, only to crumble into nonsensical sounds.

Beth tells the paramedics about medications I am taking. I am desperate to join the conversation and much to my amazement and relief the word "aspirin" somehow gets out and Beth understands. It is the first sign that I have not been completely shut out from the world.

A paramedic stands over me.

"Can you tell me your name?"

"When were you born?"

"Can you tell me what year it is?"

"Who is the president of the United States?"

I understand every word. I know the answer to every question. My brain is functioning as well as it ever has. But I cannot speak a word. I cannot tell anyone the year or my birthday or that a paralyzing fear has seized me—I will be trapped in a nonfunctioning body for the rest of my life.

More EMTs and paramedics arrive. Someone sticks an IV in my arm. EKG leads are placed. I try—and fail—to tell them about my allergy to surgical tape, which for some reason seems important at the time. Someone shines a flashlight in my eyes.

They ask if I can stand. I cannot. Strong arms grab me on either side and help me to the stretcher. I glance about the room, trying to take in the sights and smells and I am thinking *Will I ever see this again?*

I feel great sadness that I may never say good-bye to my boys or see them or touch them again.

The cool night air feels good, a peculiar contradiction now. I was wrapped in a blanket but still cold and shivering.

They roll me out across the gravel of the driveway toward the ambulances whose lights flicker eerily in our neighborhood. I am so attuned to the senses that still operate I find myself mesmerized by the sound of the crunching gravel beneath the stretcher's wheels.

They load me into the back of the brightly lit ambulance. Beth rides shotgun up front.

Two EMTs ride in the back. One sits at my side, not speaking, busy with the task of keeping me alive. The other, who says a good friend is a patient of mine, talks to me quietly, trying to put me at ease.

The double doors slam shut and we're moving. The siren begins to wail.

I look at my reflection in the glass of the ambulance's back doors. I think I look the same as I always did, not like someone who's having a stroke.

The lights outside go by quickly as I try to figure out where we are. I cannot stop thinking that I would love to be riding in a car with the windows down, the cool desert air rushing at my face.

I see the tall brick walls of the hospital and I know we are nearing the ER. How many times I have walked here to see patients, hoping that the situation is not as grave as thought, hoping the patient can be seen and sent home quickly. I worked in this ER years ago and when I am wheeled in, I search for familiar faces, but see none. It has been awhile since I last walked into this part of the hospital. Even the inside has been remodeled beyond my recognition.

It is Sunday, 2:08 A.M.

I am wheeled into a sterile white examination room, obviously used for "codes," patients like me, deemed to be in serious trouble. I look at the reinforced glass in the windows separating my room from the other side. The curtains are drawn and I cannot see out, but on my side I can read the words on the glass, changing with each window:

02__L-m__by__
Medication Dose Time
IV Fluid Rate
Defibrillation

Beth puts her arms around me and holds me. She doesn't deserve this, I think. Why must she go through all this again?

An ER physician comes in and orders a head CT. I cannot take my eyes off the clock. I need to keep track of how much time is passing. It is very important to me. But I don't know why.

At 3:30 A.M., I am rolled into the CT scanner room. As I lie on the cold metal table in the scanner's doughnut hole, I look up and see a familiar face. I am no stranger to CT scans, but I'm still surprised to see him staring back at me—a cat on a poster, fixed so that a patient flat on his back sees it as he is moved inside the scanner. The cat dangles precariously from a tree branch. Below him, the words: "Hang In There."

Back in the ER cubicle later, a neurologist comes by. The CT is negative. Good news, but I am having a panic attack. I cannot sit still. My mind seems calm, but my arms and legs want to move of their own accord. I am disconnected from them and cannot control their constant motion.

A cardiologist comes in. He listens to my heart and lungs, reviews my thick, complicated record. As with the ER doctor, I recognize him but can't remember his name. He thinks I have suffered a TIA—a transient ischemic attack, which in the long run is potentially good news. It is a sudden loss of neurological function with complete recovery usually within 24 hours.

Given the evidence—my speech was returning rapidly—I don't argue with the diagnosis. It sounds good to me.

Around six o'clock in the morning, I am wheeled into a hospital room—Room 781. I'm back on the seventh floor, the CCU, in the same room I had occupied on three previous occasions. Strange to say, but it is comforting to be in a familiar place, even this one.

Within two hours of coming to the ER, my symptoms improve dramatically, and then deteriorate. My speech becomes garbled again, the right side of my face droops. Forty minutes later, I improve again and by the time I'm moved to the CCU, I can at least speak and respond to questions. I can get up to go to the bathroom on my own, but I'm unsteady and lightheaded. Nonetheless, I am determined to be independent, but the effort eventually took more time than I liked. It would be several weeks before I could hold a pen to write.

Heparin drips into my veins. Beth is at my side always. Word gets out in church later that Sunday morning and I am again blessed by the prayers of the congregation. Visitors come to the hospital.

The Presbyterian Hospital nurses are wonderful, but the inevitable exception to the rule makes an appearance. As usual, there are problems with the IVs because the Takayasu's has toughened my veins. Like so many IV starters before her, one nurse's inflated confidence gives me pause. She announces that I have "great veins" and that the IV insertion will be a snap. I tell her it will not be a snap and I explain my history. She lectures me on being too negative and proceeds. After repeated attempts at the IV insertion, she gives up, leaving the room while grumbling about people who have low pain thresholds.

Beth stays the night.

I am in the hospital four more days, feeling better each day, getting more impatient to leave each day, and grateful again for friends and the hospital's good nursing staff, who conspire to smuggle in a hospital VCR for Beth and I to use. Designated for "patient education" videos, the VCR on those nights is used for scary movies accompanied by non-hospital popcorn.

On the fourth day, my coagulation times still keep me in the hospital and I resort to my physician's insider status in order to get out. No patient would ever be allowed to make the arguments I make, but I make them nonetheless. I persuade the physicians to discharge me, agreeing to daily doctors' visits and lab work until I am within the therapeutic coagulation range.

Before I leave, a neurologist spends forty-five minutes with us, going over everything in detail. The consensus remains that I have suffered an ischemic event, but no one knows if it was caused by a blood clot or inflammation from the Takayasu's. The best guess is a clot.

Strokes range from minor to devastating and the TIA is the mildest form, sometimes so fleeting that the victim isn't even aware it has occurred. This brings some small comfort, but I now was on the bad side of the statistics. Having suffered a TIA, I substantially increased the likelihood of having a more damaging stroke within a year.

I go home on Thursday, the fifth day. The next Monday I am back at work.

CHAPTER SEVENTEEN

Thursday
July 24, 1997

I worked all day Monday and Wednesday. I continue to experience fatigue and am having some problem with lightheadedness and my writing (I still have trouble holding the pen). Overall, I am feeling stronger than I have for a month.

I spoke to the medical students again today. I get a sense of weariness from them. Even though they have been on the ward for only a short time, I am already sensing discouragement and disillusionment. I ask myself how this can happen so quickly, then realize that I, too, have been down this path. I am saddened that they are so isolated in their pursuits.

I want to support their desire to care. It is this spirit that needs nurturing because it is this spirit that can reach out to others in need in a way technology can never correct.

Another summer monsoon storm has blown in. Every afternoon the skies cloud over. The heat of the day intensifies under the smothering blanket. Rain arrives as a few tracing droplets that evaporate the instant they strike. I look skyward each day expecting a downpour to refresh the air and cool us.

I am searching again for the "routine," the mundane chores of everyday life that have become a holy grail to me. But there is nothing mundane in the betrayal of my body. I no longer trust it.

I awake in the middle of the night now, my stomach knotted in fear, memories of the TIA flooding my thoughts. I lie in bed and survey a newly important checklist—arms moving, fingers flexing, legs moving, feet okay, brain functioning, thoughts clear.

I remind myself that the episode was isolated and in all likelihood will not return. Then each night, I get into bed wondering if I will awake paralyzed and speechless.

Thursday
August 7, 1997

The boys restarted their music lessons this week. We all crowded into a back room to hear them play. David has started reading music better even after a six-week layoff. Andy is more confident with his viola. They are quite good. They persist when we ask and they get better and better all the time. I wasn't able to stick to music when I was their age. I'm impressed that they can do it.

Thursday
August 11, 1997

I can hear Andy practice on his new guitar. He has had three lessons so far and he is impatient, wanting to move forward and play pieces from the bands on his CDs.

I am a terrible volleyball player now. Rusty, out of shape, not moving well, not going to the ball, not setting up passes like I used to, not spiking the ball with authority—but playing!

After more than six months away, I joined ten other guys from the group that played together for so many years. It brought a feeling of being complete again. The flesh may not be willing, but the spirit and memory are. At least I knew in which direction to go even if I couldn't get there when I wanted to. It took almost four days to stop feeling sore after playing that day, but I felt calm and relaxed, as if a tightened spring had somehow been unwound.

At work, a new patient came to the clinic with his wife. He claimed to have suffered from Chronic Fatigue Syndrome, although he brought no supporting information with him. He also claimed to have fibromyalgia, insomnia, lymphadenopathy and "phantom" joint pains, all the while appearing large and robust. He said his symptoms began eight years ago and he has been incapacitated since.

As I listened to him, I was struck by how well he described many of the same symptoms I have had over the years. I struggled with his description and his wife's, which sounded to me almost too-ready confirmation of his plight. Having gone through my own battles, I fought back the doubt that began creeping into my mind about the story I was hearing. I had the feeling my new patient was being less than truthful. He adamantly refused to involve himself in Chronic Fatigue Syndrome support groups. Then came what I believe was the real reason for my new patient's visit—he wanted Ativan, a habit-forming tranquilizer. My new patient had come in search of drugs.

Having experienced symptoms that had been vague and not receiving helpful answers from physicians, I knew what it was like to be desperate for those answers. Yet I still doubted these people sitting before me, telling me a tale of sickness that suffered its own credibility symptoms. They struck a raw nerve and already I anticipated disappointment if the tale they told was a deception.

I asked him for a medical record release to obtain documentation of his diagnosis and previous treatments. He said he would provide it. I never saw him again.

Two days later, I sat in my back yard, watching the other side of the human nature coin—two friends, people of courage and faith I admire like few others. Their son suffers from muscular dystrophy. He could walk as a young child, but the wasting disease has taken that and almost everything else from him. In a wheelchair now, he has control only of a small amount of his fingers; his parents feed him and dress him. He gets thinner as the days go by and his condition worsens, but you'd never know it by talking to him. Smiling always, he would sooner talk to you about his political science studies than anything. How difficult it must be for all of them. This family has such strength. I feel blessed to witness it.

Sunday
August 31, 1997

Today is our 13th anniversary. I am thankful I am here to celebrate it. I love Beth more each day. It seems impossible to imagine life without her.

This week has been unusually busy. Physically, I have felt better than I have felt for months, a phenomenon that lasted all of one day before giving way to the fatigue and soreness that have become constant companions.

But I remember the energy and enthusiasm of that one day. My body was loose; I had no stiffness. I remembered feeling this way years ago. Now that I have experienced how good I can feel, I'm more like an addict in search of a high. I yearn for more "great" days.

Tuesday
September 16, 1997

I lie awake at 2:30 in the morning. I feel low and distressed, questioning my role as a father and a husband. Am I loving my family enough? Am I doing enough? A sense of despair filled me as I sensed that time is slipping by for me to be with them. I love them so much and I wonder how the events of the past two years have affected my relationship with them.

Andy comes home telling me about his work at school. I find myself doing just what I don't want to do, nagging and threatening, when I should be encouraging. I so want him to do well.

Sunday
September 28, 1997

Achy, chilled and stiff. Last night, I awoke frequently in a sweat and had to change my bedclothes, which were drenched.

The signs that I was headed downhill again came for weeks. Beth and I went shopping in Santa Fe. Standing at a counter and talking to a shop clerk became impossible. I couldn't tolerate it. I became lightheaded and had to sit down. My heart was not pumping efficiently and my blood pooled in the lower extremities. My heart no longer had the strength to overcome gravity.

One night, as Beth and I worked in the kitchen preparing dinner, my heart began pounding in my chest. Beth was at the stove, her back turned to me. I slipped out into the garage. My stethoscope was in the car, always handy for a clandestine physical exam. I could hear Beth calling to me from the kitchen, wondering where I was. Her voice faded as she went off in the wrong direction through the house looking for me.

I must have lost track of time or become too intent on listening to my heart because I was surprised when I looked up and there she was in the garage, standing only a few feet from me. It was a moment of understanding for each of us. Neither of us spoke.

Beth took the stethoscope ear pieces from me. She knew what she was going to hear. I held the diaphragm against my chest and she listened for a long minute. She put her arms around me and we held each other. Then we went back to the kitchen and called the boys to the dinner table.

Tuesday
October 7, 1997

I will be seeing Dr. Cochran this morning. I've been aware of a slow deterioration of my energy levels and a greater persistent pounding of my heart over the past two to three weeks. Exercise has held less appeal to me and when I do exert myself, I have felt more weary and tire more easily. I've recognized many of the symptoms from before, but once again my denial mechanisms have been strong.

Sleep has been more difficult as I lie awake in the early morning hours listening to the rushing of blood and the beating of my heart.

A small channel has developed at the attachment of the homograft into the ventricle. This is not a leak, however, but the pressure has deformed the cusp of the valve. Coaptation of the cusp is impaired and leakage back into the heart occurs.

A third surgery looms.

Thoughts turn to love, not fear. I worry about the boys and pray this will pass easily. I am so thankful for all the love that surrounds me.

Angel Fire renews me. The northern New Mexico mountain peaks are like old friends—Agua Fria, Baldy, Wheeler, the state's highest at 13,161 feet. The Moache Utes named Angel Fire. The red and orange slivers of morning light became "fire of the gods" for the long ago Native Americans and when the Franciscans came with the Spanish, "fire of the gods" became "the place of the fire of the angel."

I took the kids on a long hike close to Red River, almost five miles. The walk up taxed me, but the sound of the kids' laughter echoing through the mountain forest and autumn's high altitude crispness did much to offset my fatigue. The aspens had turned to gold and the leaves that already had fallen formed a brilliant carpet that softened the trail. The return trip was easy and I found myself mentally recording each moment, committing each echo of laughter to memory, archiving the sweet smell of the forest. As much as I wanted to, I could not deny the underlying truth that I was cataloging such moments because I feared I would never see them again.

Dr. Cochran's report on the echocardiogram was good. The aorta looked well. He sent the report on to the heart surgeon in California and now we awaited his appraisal.

Beth was not happy with my conversation as we lay in bed that night in Angel Fire. I told her that if I died I wanted her to remarry. I could not stand the thought of her being lonely. I told her I just wanted some peace of mind about it. She told me not to be in such a hurry to marry her off, that she was very happy with the husband she had now.

Sunday
October 12, 1997

Snow falling on pine trees. Our last day in Angel Fire. The mountains are brushed with color— red, yellow, brown, orange, green. We hiked the Elliot Barker trail and the walk was easy for me. We sat in the cabin's living room and watched a dazzling lightning storm sweep across the mountains. I feel connected to this place.

Tuesday
October 14, 1997

I'm still waiting to find out what the heart surgeon in California thinks about my condition. Dr. Cochran has set up a cardiac catheterization for Thursday. I had planned on working two more weeks, but Wednesday will be my last day for a while.

I died on Thursday.

In a technical manner of speaking, there is no other way to put it, hyperbolic as it may sound. It was only a moment, but nonetheless, I died on Thursday, traveling to a place others have been, and returning hesitant to speak of it, yet compelled to believe.

Beth and I arrived at the hospital at six in the morning. By the time I got into the cath lab, which looks very much like an OR, I had been given 10 mg of Valium and I was feeling calm.

Beth waited in a small alcove designated for families of patients having cardiac procedures. She knew the normal time for a heart cath was about an hour and as time dragged on, her worries grew. When she saw Dr. Cochran come into the alcove still wearing his surgical scrubs, she paid it little attention. He probably had procedures all day. It was not until he got close to her that she saw his worried expression and his pale face. A rivulet of sweat trickled down his temple. He sat down beside her and took her hand.

"Steve had a little episode while he was on the table," he said.

I had experienced the most potentially lethal arrhythmia a patient can have. When Dr. Cochran advanced the catheter into the ventricle, my heart went into ventricular fibrillation. In a cardiac cath, it is one of the most serious and rare complications. Unless the fibrillation is converted quickly, it means certain death. The surgical team had to shock my heart back to its normal rhythm.

After assuring her that I was all right, Dr. Cochran took Beth into the lab to show her the video tape of the procedure. He pointed out the deformities of my aorta, the pseudoaneurysm and the problem areas where the artificial valve was attached to the aortic root. When he got to where I fibrillated, he asked the tech to pause the tape.

From that point on nothing he said registered with her. She looked at the monitor and saw only the moment of my death. She had participated in more than a hundred such "code" situations in her career as an ICU nurse; she had been part of medical teams that shocked people and pulled them back from death, just as the cath team had done for me. It was almost routine for her. But no longer.

Until she stood before that television monitor and watched me die, she had never appreciated the full meaning of those "code" moments when she raced to save a life. When you work around that degree of technology day in and day out, you lose sight of implications and consequences; and you lose sight of the burdens and responsibilities technology imposes as well.

When the cath lab team brought me out, Beth had a hard time believing her eyes. She used the word "radiant" to describe me. I was laughing and joking with the nurses. I had two perfect round circles burned on my chest where the paddles had been placed to send 200 joules of electricity through my heart to reset its rhythm.

Alone with Beth, I told her what I know sounded like an amazing story, one that defies belief, and yet I believe. I have no choice but to believe. I am not the first to tell a story like it and I will not be the last. I fully expect it to be met with skepticism, just as I fully must ask to be believed.

I was awake throughout the cardiac catheterization procedure. I talked to Dr. Cochran and the cath nurses as they worked.

Then, with no warning, I felt as if I were floating. I looked around and discovered that I was, in fact, floating toward the ceiling. I was turned so that I was looking down on people below me. I was not alarmed by any this. Quite to the contrary, I felt a peacefulness and had a sense that this was a familiar place. A bright light filled the room and as I watched the people beneath me, it clearly appeared that they were in an operating room. They were wearing scrub clothes and I could see that they were bending over a patient lying on a table and working furiously on him.

I became curious about who the patient might be and I strained to make out who it was. One of the nurses stepped away from the table and I was able to get a clearer look at the person lying there. It was me.

This discovery didn't frighten me and I can remember every detail clearly. The nurse who stepped away from the operating table had turned to grab some paddles from the defibrillator on the "crash cart" next to the table.

The next thing I knew, someone yanked hard on my left arm and I was back on the table and a voice called to me.

"Steve! Steve! Can you hear me?"

I tried to sit up. The cath technician and a nurse gently held me down.

"It's okay. You're all right," someone said.

Then it was over. I had experienced death. A few brief seconds that stretched well beyond the measure of a clock. A timeless peace I had never known.

Friday
October 17, 1997

Dr. Cochran called to inform me that I would need to go to the California Medical Center for a third heart surgery on Monday. We are leaving tomorrow. I called the Medical Center and spoke with the surgeon, who was quite kind and expressed sorrow at the news. He gave me confidence that all will go well.

Trying to prepare is difficult. The phone has been ringing off the hook. Mom, Dad and my brother, Andy, all came over.

The TGIF group has arrived. My wonderful friends have come for a prayer circle.

Saturday
October 18, 1997

Said good-bye to the boys today. I love them so much. This is the hardest part for me. They were upbeat and courageous, which gave me great relief.

CHAPTER EIGHTEEN

The first surgery had been shocking, the second extraordinary because of the spiritual events and its closeness to Christmas. The third, we told ourselves, would be all business.

We dreaded going back to the California Medical Center. We were determined to not let history repeat itself. We had been through it once, we knew what to expect, we were armed with the knowledge of the flaws in the system, we would be assertive and aggressive if we had to be. We would do what we had to do and get out. As with so many other best laid plans, our steadfast determination did little other than to antagonize the system even more than we did the first time.

Before going any farther, I must say something about the people of the Medical Center— they were, by and large, superb. The nurses, technicians, orderlies, receptionists, housekeeping, the people who are the "face" of an institution were caring and a credit to themselves and their many fields of expertise. There were exceptions, of course, but they were few.

At the top of the pyramid, however, where physicians precariously teeter in an illusion of splendid isolation, there is work to do, though there were exceptions there, too.

We lost the first battle before leaving New Mexico. I wanted to spend every minute I could with the kids at home, but the Medical Center insisted I report early in the morning on the day before surgery. We flew in the night before and stayed at the Guest

House, spending a sleepless night in a strange bed rather than having one more dinner and one more breakfast with the kids.

Then we reported to the Medical Center. And waited.

Cardiologists came by as I lay in bed, including the first (and only) physician I had met during my previous stay who understood that medicine practiced at a distance is not medicine practiced well. Two cardiologists who preceded her into my room unwittingly had proved that point.

During their visit, Beth sat at my bedside during the conversation. Neither cardiologist spoke to her, neither acknowledged her, neither so much as introduced himself to her. She might as well have been another chair in the room.

My old nemesis, the surgical consent form, made a return appearance, first in the hands of a physician who spent a long time answering questions and providing information at length. She asked if I would sign the consent form. I deferred, saying I would rather speak with the lead surgeon or one of the other surgeons directly involved in my case. She said she had no problem with that and left.

As before, though, the consent form was bequeathed to each succeeding physician and nurse who appeared in the doorway. Each asked that I sign it, most understood why I declined, two or three seemed offended that once again I was gumming up the protocol.

By nine-thirty that night I had been in bed for twelve hours. An IV delivered heparin to thin my blood. I took a shower and shaved. I ate lunch and dinner. I read newspapers from front to back. My vital signs had yet to be taken.

A second-year surgery resident came by to tell me the surgeon would not be available to speak with me until the next day, the day of the surgery. She was not able to discuss what plan the surgeon had in mind. I declined to sign the surgical consent form she offered. She was the last doctor I saw until the next morning, and with her departure came the unsettling memory of my last stay here, when miscommunication somewhere in the medical labyrinth nearly discharged me out of the ICU and onto the street.

Surgery was scheduled for 8:00 A.M. with expected transport to the operating room at 7:30. Beth, my mother, and my brother came early. Around seven o'clock a nurse-practitioner came in with the consent form. I asked about meeting with the surgeon before I signed. She left with an unsigned consent form.

At 7:45, Andy went into the hall to see if he could find someone who knew when I would be taken to surgery. He found the nurse-practitioner. She told him the surgery has been pushed back to the afternoon.

Around nine o'clock, the eminent surgeon who had operated on me the first time at the Medical Center unexpectedly appeared. Soft-spoken and polite, he explained the detailed procedure with the caveat that he would not know for sure what the situation was until my chest was opened and he could evaluate the situation.

His demeanor was markedly different from the first surgery, when he came into my room and delivered a canned performance made memorable only by its rote, mechanical nature. When he left the room this time, I was struck at how these few minutes of communication changed everything for me, the patient. My mood was elevated, I was encouraged. It took only a few minutes, a small investment of time made large by unseen dividends, and I wondered why this simple lesson is so hard for physicians to learn.

Around one o'clock in the afternoon, a nurse arrived with the consent form. We reviewed it carefully. I signed it.

Surgery began around two o'clock. I was back in the ICU by ten-thirty that night. As I struggled back to consciousness, I somehow had the presence of mind to listen for the clicking of the artificial valve in my chest. When I heard it, I relaxed. The surgeon had said he would put in an artificial valve if he found no evidence of infection or severe inflammation.

But the procedure was not without its problems. Fresh blood clots had formed in aneurysm cavities. The surgery team worried that removing them would send fragments through my arteries to the brain and trigger a stroke. But they wouldn't know until I regained consciousness. The two previous surgeries left little of the aortic root to which the surgeons might attach the new mechanical valve. The diminished aortic root forced the surgeons to anchor the valve farther down into the ventricle, where they had to attach it dangerously close to electrical conduction pathways carrying impulses that stimulate the heart to beat. I developed heart block in the OR that required help from a pacemaker.

The next morning Beth came to the ICU. I was still intubated and having trouble breathing. The surgery residents couldn't figure why. But Beth knew. She gently made a suggestion. The two surgery residents not so gently blew her off.

To be shown up by a patient's wife was unthinkable, never mind that she knew what she was talking about. In her nursing career, Beth had spent years working with ventilator patients in ICUs. She looked at the size of my endotracheal tube and at my blood gas results and knew the tube was too small.

She asked the surgery residents about this. They ignored the question. An hour later, the attending pulmonary physician came in, examined me and pronounced the tube to be too small, though there was good reason for its smallness. My vocal chords had been damaged in the previous surgery and more room was needed for another instrument used to view the back of my heart during surgery.

Nonetheless, a suggestion from an experienced healthcare professional was found not worthy of the most perfunctory discussion. Why was Beth's inquiry ignored? An assault on turf?

An incursion by an interloper? An interfering patient's wife out of her depth? Only the two surgery residents know why.

The doctor parade then began—the cardio thoracic fellow, the second-year surgical resident, the cardiologist and the cardiology fellow, more cardiologists; then the nurse-practitioner, the next nurse-practitioner, the clinical nurse specialist, the next clinical nurse specialist—all well-trained professionals, competent and in command of each of their varied specialities, and few, if any, talking to one another.

All had something to say, all had something to write, all had something to order, and too often the orders conflicted. One service ordered X and an hour later another countermanded that order with Y. Medications were stopped that shouldn't have been stopped, confusion and conflicting orders caused delays in starting medications that should have been started.

Continuity of care becomes a casualty and the patient is lost in the War of the Attendings.

The Medical Center gives patients a manifesto in which the rights of the patient are itemized. It lists fourteen, such as "knowing the names and roles of physicians and non-physicians who will see you" and "receive enough information about treatments and procedures to make informed decisions concerning your medical care" (which my Albuquerque physicians, who simply gave up trying to pry information out of the Medical Center, would have found ironic).

One item in particular resonated with me in the days after surgery—"participate actively in decisions regarding medical care. To the extent permitted by law, this includes the right to refuse treatment."

In the hours prior to surgery, I told each doctor who came in my room (and took my history repeatedly) that I had stopped taking prednisone, that under no circumstances did I want prednisone, that I had found prednisone to be deleterious to my healing.

Yet someone wrote in my progress notes that I was still taking prednisone and I was given two large doses of a steroid in the operating room.

There were other problems. The team had difficulty getting my anticoagulation therapy adjusted. I had a mechanical valve again and I was started back on anticoagulants—heparin and Coumadin. They couldn't get my bleeding times within an acceptable range and couldn't figure out why, although at least one or two of the other medications prescribed for me interfered with Coumadin. I tried to discuss this with them, but to no avail. They thought the best way to handle it was to keep increasing the heparin and Coumadin doses.

I asked Beth to stay with me as much as possible. I needed an advocate and a watchdog. I was not in a position to fend for myself. She was there by seven in the morning and did not leave until around eleven at night. But the night before I was discharged I suggested she leave around nine o'clock and get some much needed rest.

I drifted off to sleep as soon as Beth left, awaking again around nine-thirty. Something warm and wet trickled down my left arm. I thought I might have been dreaming and though curious, dismissed it.

Then I felt the sensation again, this time on my right arm; then again down the side of my chest; then underneath me, as if something wet were pooling in the sheets. Awake now, I looked at my arm. Blood ran from an old IV puncture site. I pulled back the sheets. Blood pooled in the bed. I quickly surveyed as much of my body as I could. Blood dripped from every wound, every old IV site.

If this is happening on the outside, I thought, *what is happening on the inside?*

I frantically pressed the button on my nurse call light. No one came. I pressed it again and again. No one came. I grabbed the phone and called Beth. She had just gotten into bed and was half-asleep. I told her what was happening. She called the nurses' station and told whoever answered to get a nurse to my room immediately, then she ran the two blocks to the hospital.

When Beth walked into my room, she saw a nurse changing my dressings. Blood and serous fluid stained the bed. The nurse had notified the resident, who gave orders to check my "bleeding times." In the weeks after I was discharged, I asked a friend who practiced at the Medical Center to see if she could obtain any records of these bleeding times. She found a few progress notes and lab numbers. One is chilling.

An APPT (Activated Partial Thromboplastin Time) measures the specific blood clotting mechanism prolonged by heparin therapy. The reference range—the time it takes for a clot to form—is 24.2 to 37.8 seconds. The goal for a patient on heparin is 1.5 times greater than that. Given the benefit of the doubt, the upper range would be 55 seconds.

I was unable to obtain the APPT numbers drawn at the time of the incident, but a measurement taken four hours earlier showed 180 seconds, a "panic value." I can only assume that four hours later, the number would have been even worse because the heparin continued to be infused. Those lab reports should have been reported immediately and adjustments should have been made in the heparin dose.

The doctors had overshot the mark on my heparin. It was dangerously high. Finally, someone ordered the heparin to be discontinued.

At about two in the morning, a nurse practitioner came into the room and I spoke of my concern about the heparin. She repeatedly asked if I was refusing the heparin until it became clear to me that the questions had more to do with legal considerations than it did about any worry I might have about the drug therapy. She suggested I write a letter of complaint and gave me the names and addresses of Medical Center administrators. It was the best she could do after I repeatedly asked who I could talk to about it.

At no time did a doctor ever come to check on me. Beth stayed the night. Neither of us slept.

My blood numbers improved as the morning wore on. Discharge was scheduled for noon, which was fine with me, as it would have prevented a room charge for another full day.

A clinical nurse specialist stopped by and we had a long, detailed talk about the events of my stay: the prednisone therapy; confusions regarding medications on my chart; the rheumatologist suggesting I start methotrexate while surgeons and other specialists counseled against it, a confusion never cleared up; and questions I had about Coumadin.

The nurse spent a lot of time listening and discussing these things with me and then became the second person in only hours to make the same suggestion—write a letter to an administrator. I asked if she would consider writing an incident report so the circumstances could be reviewed and corrective measures could be instituted. She would not.

Twenty minutes before noon, one last obstacle appeared. A nurse said I couldn't leave until blood tests done at six that morning were reviewed by a resident. There was no hint that anyone would review them anytime in the near future. I was ready to sign out of the hospital "AMA" (against medical advice). I told the nurse someone needed to call the resident and tell him to review the labs immediately. Arrangements were made, a doctor looked at the results, and at 12:05 I was in a wheelchair, headed toward an elevator.

I imagine that somewhere in the many notes written about me is one mentioning a hostile and uncooperative patient. I suspect that much of the time the medical staff did not know what to make of us. But hostility is not my nature, nor is it Beth's. We had decided beforehand that based on experience we had to ask direct questions in order to get information. If that information was not forthcoming when doctors and nurses came to my room, we asked what their roles were and what plans they had made for my treatment. We were much more assertive than we had been previously and there is no doubt in my mind that it annoyed many of my providers. I am sure many had not encountered that kind of interaction with a patient before.

Regardless of our newfound assertiveness, explanations too often did not come. They should have.

CHAPTER NINETEEN

Home again, a sense of escape, surviving one more time to marvel at New Mexico's crisp fall air, see its striking colors, walk into my sanctuary and feel safe behind its thick mud walls. I look up at the *vigas,* hand-peeled tree trunks made into beams that run a few feet apart under the ceiling throughout the house; I run my fingers across the exposed wood of doorways and hallways, letting my amateur carpenter's fingers linger on the grain; I find the nicks gouged from collisions with children and toys and furniture being squeezed from one room to another.

We weren't home long when the boys returned from school. It felt so good to put my arms around them. Initially, I thought my return had dispelled their fears, but that moment of relief didn't last the night. David's eyes belied any sense of comfort I entertained.

Beth started a fire in the family room fireplace and I settled into the big, overstuffed chair. It was a Wednesday night. Homework and books spread across the heavy pine table in the dining room. Beth and the boys carried on a running conversation, them at the table with their books and papers, Beth working in the kitchen. Andy had a stock market project at school in which the students had been allotted imaginary money to invest any way they chose and he was delighted that his stocks were doing better than the ones we actually invested in. David worked as he always did—concentrating on the task at hand, asking his mother questions, telling his brother he talked too much.

After dinner came music practice. David already was starting to work on his Christmas recital piece and Andy worked on a Rondo by Henri Ernst. Then it was showers and bed for the boys, but first hugs and kisses from Mom, then a hug from me. But no kiss. My sons had reached the stage at which certain indignities could no longer be suffered.

Small lines of worry etched around David's deep brown eyes. Naturally quiet and withdrawn, he could not hide the uneasiness in his eyes. Even exuberant Andy was subdued. My sickness had changed their lives. At school, they hated to see an unexpected family member or friend in the pick-up area waiting for them because it meant that Dad was in the hospital again. Beth always made sure they had money in their pockets for emergencies. She never had to tell them not to spend it frivolously and they never did. They understood its purpose. We never knew when they might get stranded somewhere and have to take a cab or find a ride home.

They had given up going out for sports because no sooner would they start something than I would get sick and they would have to drop out. They attended schools outside of our neighborhood and driving them to visit friends from school was often impossible, so they learned to entertain themselves at home. David became a Lego collector and builder.

We rarely talked about these things. The boys resisted it. But that first night home, I saw all the fearful questions in David's eyes. Ten years old is so young to have such things etched into a face.

Twelve years old is no better, as I would learn when Beth and I went to the school for Andy's parent-teacher conference. The commons was decorated with student work. The semester focus had been on families and researching their roots, kids making discoveries about themselves as individuals and finding where they fit in. They had done individual projects that involved drawing a time line of significant events in their lives. The time line stretched out in young handwriting along long rolls of butcher paper. It contained the expected—births, brothers and sisters, learning to walk, ride a bike, making the soccer team, getting a new puppy.

We read several before coming to Andy's. It began the way the others did. Then came more recent entries:

"1995—My Dad got sick."

"1996—My best friend died. [A boy who died of cancer.] My Dad got sick."

"1997—My Dad got sick."

There were no more entries. I hoped none of the other parents in the room saw me before I had wiped away all my tears.

Friday
October 31, 1997

Cousin David, the cardiologist, warned me I would experience more fatigue. I think that my lack of sleep and the stress of surgery is catching up with me. I've felt more weary today, having to work harder at walking or doing my breathing exercises.

Stayed home with Beth on Halloween and handed out treats. It was good to see the kids stuffing themselves with candy.

Wednesday
November 19, 1997

It's been nineteen days since my last entry. I've often thought about writing, but have found it difficult to do. Beth thinks I'm more depressed this time around, and though I don't entirely agree, I must admit that my general outlook is less enthusiastic or optimistic. I think I am still just as motivated as before to recover, but many questions are yet to be addressed. I have a lot of confusion about what to do.

I walked the bosque trail today. The sun shone brilliantly and warmed me enough to remove my jacket. I still suffer from

significant fatigue and my right neck and upper back hurt ter-
ribly. I'm having difficulty raising my right arm. I've noticed an
unpleasant rubbing to my left lower chest around the chest tube
site. My suspicion is that my left lower lung and diaphragm are
moving more, so I guess this rub is also a good indication of
healing.

Tomorrow marks the one month anniversary of my surgery.

A realization clouded my mind, then darkened my outlook even more: I could not help Andy with his homework. I sat with him at the dining table, working on a math problem, and it became clear to me that I could not solve it. I didn't know why. I couldn't explain it. I wondered if some permanent brain damage had been done in the last surgery or through a combination of surgeries—all the anesthesia, all the times I was on bypass, all the times the blood flow to my brain was interrupted or re-routed. If there was damage, was it permanent? Even if it was temporary, how could I work? How could I use my critical thinking with my patients when I could not solve my son's math homework? I wondered who and what I had become. If I was no longer Dr. Steven Hsi, who was I?

One afternoon, as I sat on the back patio watching Beth stuff leaves into plastic bags, the question seemed to come of its own will. I had not planned on asking it, but suddenly, there it was.

"Have you noticed anything wrong with the way I think? With my thought processing, I mean," I asked Beth.

She came over to me and sat in the chair next to mine. She took my hand and I cannot imagine how difficult it must have been for her to say what she did.

"Yes."

I decided not to make any big plans until next year. The thought of returning to work caused me fear and worry. I didn't know when I would be up to the demands of a medical practice. Certainly not then and not for a while. My workaholic days were over; my insistence on doing too much too soon had been tamed by the demands of recovery. I preferred to stay home with Beth and the boys in any case. I was never much of a social animal to begin with and even less so now.

I couldn't be still. I was restless and couldn't stay focused on anything for long. Reading was difficult, writing even more so. My mind wandered in all directions. I felt rudderless. By early December I had reached a plateau. My energy levels waxed and waned. The restlessness continued and I was impatient. I was surprised that I was having trouble, though my son, David, did his best to drag me out of my funk.

About two weeks before Christmas, it snowed heavily, leaving the streets icy and treacherous. School was canceled and the boys had the day off. That evening David wanted to go outside for a walk. I was anchored in the overstuffed chair in front of the fire and I had no intention of moving, most certainly not to go outside in the snow and ice. I gave him one excuse after another, but David would have none of it. I surrendered. All of us bundled up and went out into the night.

It was cold but not bitterly so. The new snow glittered in the light coming from homes and streetlights. The hush of the snow muffled the sounds of cars and barking dogs. Four or five inches had piled up and it was snowing again as we walked. We walked the length of our street and then along one of the many irrigation ditches that run through Albuquerque's valley neighborhoods. The wet snow clung to the tree branches and they dipped to the ground under the weight of it. Beth and I held hands. Andy walked alongside us. David raced ahead, sliding in the snow, turning back to run to us and then racing off again when he could no longer contain himself. A white halo encircled the corner streetlight.

Tuesday
Jan. 6, 1998

I lost my memory today. It happened while at the library. I had gone to return and re-check out some books, but soon after arriving I went blank. It happened so quickly. I knew something was wrong and managed to grab the books, get into the car and drive home. I felt disoriented and struggled to recall what happened. The pieces are not coming together very well. I feel tired and still disassociated somehow. Things still seem a little fuzzy. Was this a TIA?

I talked to Dr. Cochran, my cardiologist, about the memory loss. He checked and said the heart sounded good, which lifted my spirits enough to make reservations to travel to Hawaii for the kids' spring break.

I started woodworking again, which delighted my soul. I had never thought such peace could be found flowing through my hands. Lost in the woodworking world, I became unaware of the cold in the garage or the time and it often took the ringing of the telephone or return of Beth and the boys to jolt me out of the trance.

The routine of the lives around me slowly permeated mine. We spent a few days in Angel Fire; Andy auditioned for a play; we began moving the boys into separate bedrooms and I found out they and Beth are much more efficient than I am at dispatching drawings and old school papers and toys. I want to save it all, seeing memories in every piece of flotsam. I had always been a pack rat. Even more so now.

Peaceful moments came but couldn't be created—driving home after dropping off the boys at school or lost in woodworking. Yet when I looked for those moments, when I tried to make them happen, they escaped me.

Wednesday
January 21, 1998

Lately, I've been awakened in the early hours of nights. I lie terrified that I might have another stroke. I fear going to sleep and being paralyzed or speechless when I wake up. I listen to the loud pounding of my heart and test my movements. Not that there is any explanation for the anxiety. I know I am more fearful than before.

Monday
February 23, 1998

Winter (what there has been of it) is yielding to spring and the peonies and daffodils push upward to bring color to the browns and grays. Buds appear on the apricot tree. Our cats sit steadfastly by the windows, looking out at the birds building their nests.

We spent ten days in Hawaii over the boys' spring vacation. We stayed away from the city and the crowds as much as possible and the days were lazy and relaxing, except for one, on which I saw my oldest son grow before my eyes.

Andy, David and I went snorkeling. David was first to get his equipment on and before I knew it, he was far offshore. The current grabbed him and though he was a strong swimmer in his own right, he began screaming at us for help. I couldn't hear him over the pounding surf, but I clearly saw he was in trouble. By the time I swam out to him, I was exhausted. He had pulled off his mask and snorkel and was struggling to swim back toward shore. I grabbed him around the waist so he could put his mask and snorkel back on.

But now I was in trouble. I had no energy and I was so tired I could hardly move. The current pulled us back out. Suddenly, Andy appeared. I hadn't seen him get in the water and his appearance shocked me. He didn't try to grab David, but pushed him along in front of him until David was free of the current and could make his way back. Now that I didn't have to hold onto David, I could swim back, too. Moments later, David and I lay shivering and exhausted on the beach.

It seemed my oldest son was leaving boyhood behind and becoming a young man and I could not rid myself of the idea that the torch somehow had been passed long before its time. Andy did for me what I could not do for myself. He was thirteen years old. We decided we'd had enough of the beach for the day.

Back home from Hawaii, I again attended the Thursday meetings of the Spirituality in Healthcare group, but I found myself growing distant from them. The group had veered from the path of spirituality and healthcare and had become a kind of support group for people exploring alternative spiritual paths. I had no interest in Hindi Prana or "synchronicity." I tried to feel a part of it, but I couldn't get "connected" (a favorite term used at these sessions).

I examined myself to see why I felt uncomfortable and challenged by them. They are pleasant people and I liked them, but their enlightenment came with a sense of superiority. It reminded me too much of experiences with born-again Christians who see their narrow path to salvation as the only way. The Thursday group seemed to be covering up its own pain by wanting to project an image of greater insight and under-standing. When I question them, I feel the outsider, the unen-lightened one.

Doctors fear exposing their weaknesses to their patients. They know there isn't a cure for every disease, yet most still think it is their duty to keep their patients alive at all costs, often caus-ing great suffering for the patient and his family. They do not cope with failure well; they aren't prepared for it. In the eyes of many physicians, losing a patient is failing. When they sense they have lost the battle, they distance themselves from the patient; some become angry because of the profound emotions triggered in them by the patient's situation, leaving the patient feeling confused and emotionally abandoned.

My role as a doctor is to share information with the patient, to help the patient participate in decisions; my job is to demystify the science, define problems and then help the patient through the planning and decision making. We are missing the boat when we do not involve the patients in their own care. They can be a powerful resource. We need to draw on patients' strengths and abilities, and this includes their spiritual beliefs and support systems, all of which runs counter to the distancing messages physicians-in-training receive either implicitly or explicitly.

Physicians must yield their positions as remote authority figures. Their remoteness limits them. But in order to do this, the doctor has to be aware of his patients' beliefs.

It's hard for a physician to stand by and watch a patient die. To do that, physicians must confront their sense of helplessness and their own feelings about death. There is a place in our busy lives for what can be learned from spending a little time with a dying patient. When I have taken such time, I have seen painful things and good things. My patients have expressed their anger and their hopes to me. And I hoped with them, for a cure, for and end to their pain, for peace.

I laughed with them, too. They faced death, as I had faced it. We had nothing to lose by laughing. Quirky, eccentric, genuinely funny—my patients were a joy to be with and I cherish the time spent with them.

Sick people open a window into their lives and sometimes their souls. Most doctors slam the window shut as quickly as possible. I wish they would not. That window is a precious gift, a sacred trust. I know the loneliness of the critically and chronically ill. I know the sound of that window being slammed shut.

The days passed quickly. Beth and I felt my mental acuity had returned by early March and I was back at work. At first, I spent only a few hours a day in the office with administrative work, but I found myself being drawn to my patients. Soon I was back on a regular schedule.

I loved seeing my patients. They rejuvenated me. My experience as a patient broadened the scope of my practice and I looked forward to each day eagerly, but as I reflected on it, it became clear to me that something larger played a role, too—the idea of community. I found myself coming back to its importance repeatedly. I had been embraced by so many communities: my church, the fellowship group, my family, my patients and even their churches. I found myself awakening again to my faith in God, for it was in these communities that I found Him.

I wrote a letter to the congregation at First Presbyterian.

"Sometimes we go to church and are not aware of the spiritual bond we all share," I wrote. "We pray but we don't see the results of our prayers. We sit in church hearing about wonderful deeds and miracles and we ask ourselves why we never witness these acts. Perhaps we don't really believe that they occurred or that God used up all his miracles in earlier ages. Maybe we have become too sophisticated to be fooled by this or maybe we just cannot believe in fairy tales. I certainly had my doubts. Coming from a scientific background, I found it difficult to accept how God could do these fantastic works. Surely, humankind would eventually be able to explain all of this with our scientific methods and principles.

"However, I can attest that God is ever present in our lives. Miracles have happened to us. God has heard your prayers and has responded. I am grateful for the opportunity that I have to live amongst you, sharing the love which I have been blessed to receive. But I have had glimpses of the great Spirit which has spoken to me in my illness and I know that death is part of our greater journey to the Church Triumphant.

"True healing is greater than good physical health. True healing is, in fact, a call to love one's self and others and God.

"From 'The Song of Prayer,' an extension of 'A Course in Miracles': 'If there has been true healing , this can be the form in which death comes when it is time to rest a while from labor gladly done and gladly ended. No, we go in peace to freer air and gentler climate, where it is not hard to see the gifts we gave were saved for us. For Christ is clearer now; His vision more sustained in us; His voice, the word of God, more certainly our own.'"

Monday
April 27, 1998

It snowed yesterday. Huge, heavy flakes fell and for a brief moment it felt like winter. The snow soon melted. Everything is green as the last white flowers of the crab apple and pear trees fell to the ground. The apricot tree next to the window where I sit is covered with early green fruit.

My mood is much like our weather. My energy comes and goes. I still get winded with little exertion and it discourages me. No chest pain or rapid heart beats beyond the expected. Just a tightness and general feeling of mild breathlessness which makes me stop doing whatever I'm doing. I'm not pushing hard and quit at the first sign of trouble.

We traveled to conferences. A seven-month checkup with Dr. Cochran went well. I played volleyball on a regular basis again. When the boys got out of school, we went to Seattle, combining business (my Family Practice re-certification) with pleasure. Only a week before leaving we had gone backpacking in Angel Fire, returned for a short work week and then left for the West Coast.

I visited an old friend from medical school and I was saddened at what I found. He had joined a large, multi-specialty group and initially enjoyed it, but with the passing years and increased managed care oversight, he became more and more disillusioned. I had seen similar stories played out in Albuquerque with other doctors. They entered medicine with bright-eyed ambition only to find their dream just that, an illusion that never quite became reality, and what has followed is an epidemic of disillusionment among physicians.

They are stuck, enjoying the money they get and the freedom from administrative burdens, but feeling trapped in jobs that give little satisfaction. My old medical school friend separates himself from his family, his greatest asset to harmony. My heart goes out to them all. I pray that they realize they have options, choices their families will support.

Doctors are supposed to be the healers, the support for patients with illness. But too often doctors find themselves without any support in their time of need, especially from their colleagues in the medical profession. The isolation is at least in part self-imposed, yet not deliberate. Because we are workaholics, we isolate ourselves, alienate ourselves from our families and friends.

Sunday
July 19, 1998

We returned from our West Coast adventure yesterday. Traveling is like a dream, our lives unaffected by work or the business of home. It's like watching the years pass by. Each time a vacation ends, I'm acutely aware of the passage of a few more ticks of the clock.

We were home only a week when we went back to the Northwest, this time to Oregon, the family traveling together. Beth and I attended a meeting in Portland, which could not have ended too soon for me. I wanted to leave the city and get out into the countryside with the boys.

Back home again, we raced through September, leaving once again in the middle of the month for the American Academy of Family Physicians conference in San Francisco. We had plenty of free time with the kids, and this would be the last trip in a while because of school schedules, so we took in the delights of our favorite city: Dim Sum in Chinatown, North Beach, Muir Woods, musicals, Alcatraz, museums, and David's side trip to heaven— Jackie Chan's autograph in the Borders bookstore.

Wednesday
October 7, 1998

I'm more reserved this year as my anniversary date for the last surgery approaches. It's been a good year of recovery without any major events to suggest problems. Except last week, when I finally broke down and started antibiotics for a sinus infection. I became more concerned as unusual symptoms arose—a brief vertigo and painful tendonitis to my left thigh, pain in my left index finger of no specific etiology. I even noticed brief memory defects having to do with forgetting patients I had seen only the day before.

As usual, I fear being an alarmist. Right now, I'm convinced it's just a virus, something "going around."

I was playing volleyball when my foot began to hurt, a deep, burning sensation that quickly moved into my ankle and calf. I had never felt anything like it before. I sat out a couple of games and then started playing again. Within minutes, the burning returned. When I got home I examined my left foot. It was significantly cooler than the right and I couldn't feel my pulse in it.

I recognized the symptoms immediately—arterial embolism, a blood clot. The next day I was back in the hospital.

I wanted to hold off doing anything until I could speak with Dr. Cochran, but at five o'clock the next morning I was wide awake and my calf hurt. Beth wanted to drive me to the Emergency Room, but I told her I could do it myself. We thought about calling my parents or friends to come over to be with the kids, but we didn't want the boys finding out Dad was back in the hospital from someone other than Beth. She would come to the hospital after the boys woke up and she told them what was happening.

As I drove to the Presbyterian Hospital emergency room, the fearful guessing began again: Was it a clot? Was it a progression of Takayasu's? If a clot, where did it come from? A pseudoaneurysm? The valve problem?

The answer came in an angiogram: a clot blocking the main artery behind the knee that supplied blood to the lower leg.)

They tried "clot busters" first, heparin and urokinase, a powerful anti-coagulant. A catheter was inserted through the femoral artery in my groin and threaded through to the area of the clot.

Beth had not yet arrived as the doctors explained the risks of hemorrhage and stroke, explanations I had heard on many occasions before. She came in just as they started the procedure. A technician directed her to the radiology procedure room. She saw the X-rays mounted on view boxes. The blockage was evident.

The doctors had held up the procedure until she could get there. They explained everything that was happening. They asked about the boys and how Beth was doing.

The contrast to the California Medical Center was striking. While it is true that I knew these doctors and some knew Beth, I cannot help but look at the experience in the light of what happened at Medical Center. It took only minutes for them to explain the situation to Beth. It took less than a minute to inquire about our family. That minimal effort changed the dynamic dramatically and made all the difference in the world to each of us.

They tried to suck the clot through the catheter, but failed. They tried again to dissolve it with urokinase. They discussed everything again with both of us, which included us in the decision-making process. The artery opened up but not completely. The catheter was left in place. A urokinase IV drip was begun.

I was back in the hospital again, the familiar seventh floor, the CCU.

For the next four days, I remained a prisoner of the hospital bed except for regular forays to radiology for angiograms. On the second day, the clot finally broke up and was removed. The artery cleared. I was a few days short of staying out of trouble for a whole year after surgery.

Back home, Beth gave me Lovenox injections, a low molecular weight heparin.

Normally, I would have had to stay in the hospital for anticoagulation therapy (as I had in the past), but with Lovenox on the market and Beth able to give the injections at home, I was able to escape with that and a promise to schedule the echocardiogram as an outpatient within a few days so the source of the clot could be determined.

Another problem solved. But more and more, a troubling thought forced itself into my mind, though I said nothing to Beth. There seemed to be too many signals now. I could no longer ignore them. I was running out of time.

CHAPTER TWENTY

Tuesday
October 13, 1998

Two days off, then tomorrow I return to work. My feelings of work are confused. On one hand, I love patient care and believe this is a gift that God has given me. Yet it tends to take so much out of me at times. I struggle daily with this question, not knowing what the right answer is.

Monday
October 19, 1998

We await the echocardiogram tomorrow. I tried working last week on Wednesday and Thursday. Wednesday went well, but I had great fatigue Thursday. I was perhaps a bit too eager to prove my recovery and was weary at day's end.

A patient asked if I have returned to work full-time, not knowing of my recent hospitalization. I feel guilty, almost like I have to justify the part-time nature of my work. Physically, I know this is what I must do now, if not stop practicing altogether. But I hate to feel like a quitter.

Life rumbled on in spite of my quiet protests to the contrary. Work schedules filled up, school activities kept the boys on the move, Beth worked harder than ever in the clinical trials, a long-delayed kitchen remodeling was back on track; my energy, as had become predictable now, came and went, sometimes good, sometimes not.

My one-year surgery anniversary passed by with encouraging news—the echocardiogram looked good, though no source of the blood clot behind my knee ever was found. The assortment of unexplained aches and pains continued: one in my left index finger, another in my right small toe. I tried not to read too much into them.

Beth and I attended a healing service at First Presbyterian Church. We recognized many of the forty-five people who attended—a friend ravaged by cancer, a kidney transplant patient, a man who had just recently gone through a divorce. We read Bible passages related to healing and faith. I held Beth's hand tightly and prayed for time with her.

When the service ended, we gathered in the sanctuary. Friends Lane and Marilyn Leckman came to talk with us. We always marveled at the serenity and peacefulness of Marilyn, despite the aggressive cancer that attacked and weakened her. I talked to Marilyn, Beth spoke with Lane.

Then I said to Lane and Beth, "Marilyn and I have decided that of the four of us, you two have the harder job."

In Beth's eyes I saw a refusal—*Don't tell me this now. Not now. Not yet.*

I couldn't seem to stop myself. I had thought about it daily. I was certain I would never see my sons grow to be men, never see them marry, never know my grandchildren. But my pain would end. Beth's would endure, just as Lane's would endure when Marilyn was gone. I had suffered physical pain and shouldered an emotional burden of fear and uncertainty, but I had not carried the burden alone. Beth was with me always. Even when physically separated, I felt a closeness to her I had never known before. I thought about her waking in the night to reach over and finding no one there. I thought about her being alone. I was going to God. She had the tougher days ahead.

Thanksgiving went by in a blur and soon the days grew shorter as we were swept into the Christmas rush. Not that I had anything to complain about. Our lives were less consumed with my health problems now. I had more good days than bad. Two years ago, I was blithely preparing for Christmas, feeling run down but not knowing the disaster that was occurring inside.

Old feelings and memories about that time arose all through the holidays, but I was content that there would be no undue excitement this Christmas, only fighting traffic and waiting in long lines.

Tuesday
December 29, 1998

I've had a few bad days starting around Christmas, mostly feelings of exhaustion. I've been aware of slight disequilibrium and a little more irregularity to my heartbeat. An odd experience is one of not being able to fully take in deep breaths.

Thursday
Jan 21, 1999

David and Andy are back in school. Beth and I continue working without any major break in schedule. The practice is growing and I'm feeling more confident about the future.

Monday
February 22, 1999

Every weekend this month I've had bad headaches that won't go away. Activity lessens my awareness of pain, but at rest they become more severe. I don't recall having had such frequency of headaches for many years.

Beth mentioned her sadness at our not skiing anymore. I've had to make the difficult decision that I may have to stop skiing. I am afraid of an accident, which combined with my Coumadin, could prove very serious. I share her sadness.

Beth and I went to Sundance, Utah, for a medical conference. We took two extra days for ourselves in a small cabin with an oversized fireplace. Snow crept up to the windowsills. We drank hot tea and read aloud to one another from books we brought. We talked about how perceptions determined emotions and how often those perceptions could be wrong. We talked about the wisdom of not letting anger define us, despite the bitter moments we had seen in the past few years. We talked about our gratitude for the lessons we learned and for the people God put in our lives and for the time we had together.

I felt no resignation in any of this. More an acceptance. The previous year had been frantic. As Beth's grandfather used to say, we tried to cram a quart into a pint container. It was different now. I felt at peace, though the skeptic might argue it was more capitulation than serenity. But I would disagree. I was ready to accept whatever God had in store for me. It is hard to pinpoint when I made the decision, probably after the hospitalization for the blood clot.

Regardless of its historical beginnings, I had to acknowledge reality and embrace it. My life was coming to an end, and possibly soon.

We took a long walk one night into the bitter mountain cold. When we came back to the cabin, we pulled the goose down comforter from the bed and rolled it up on the floor in front of the blazing fireplace. We lay there face to face and fell asleep.

Friday
March 5, 1999

David got on the straight A honor roll again, but I worry about my younger child, who seems so eager to please, but ill at ease around others. He is still so young. He is by and large an introvert. He enjoys his space, his own surroundings and being in his own head. This conflicts with those who are outgoing and they have difficulty understanding him. I pray that David will know he is loved for who he is and that he does not have to be someone he is not.

Sunday
March 14, 1999

A few worries about my heart. A few episodes of mild lightheadedness and fatigue. Palpitations a little more often. And is it my imagination or is my heart sounding a little louder with respect to my valve?

We've just gotten through a hectic week. We're all busy and it's a rare occasion that finds all four of us together for any extended period of time.

Friday
March 19, 1999

Still awakening with headaches in the morning. I am unsure what the symptoms are telling me. If I stand very long, I feel weak and a little queasy. Yet when I bicycled three days ago, I felt okay.

That weekend was Andy's confirmation at First Presbyterian. He had stayed at a friend's house overnight and Beth and I were to pick him up on the way to church. I was in the kitchen, making pancakes, when the phone rang. It was Andy, insisting that I put Beth on the phone. I tried to find out what was happening, but he was adamant—he wanted to talk to his mother, not me.

She came to the phone. He wouldn't tell her what had happened, only that she needed to come get him right away.

An hour later, the three of us sat in the family room. Andy told the story.

Four boys, all members of Andy's band, spent the night. After the parents had gone to bed, the boys sneaked a bottle of wine from a kitchen cupboard and drank it quickly, with the predictable result. All of them threw up. One passed out.

Andy seemed truly repentant, and truly petrified at what would come next. I couldn't blame him, given my behavior in the past. He had every right to expect an explosion of anger and a grounding that would last forever.

I told him I loved him. I told him that getting sick and throwing up was punishment enough and we agreed that he would write a letter of apology to his host's parents. Then everyone got ready for church. Except for me. I wanted very much to be there for Andy's confirmation, but I was feeling weak and tired. I went back to bed and didn't awake until Beth and the boys came home from church.

Beth said the confirmation went well. People inquired about my absence. She told them I had a virus. She said Andy had been quiet all the way home, until they turned down our street, when he said, "Wow, Mom! Two rites of passage in one day!"

They laughed all the way home. I laughed, too.

Tuesday
March 23, 1999

One busy week before Holy Week. David turns 11 on Thursday. I'm happy for him. He is acting more and more like the boy he was in pre-school—happy-go-lucky, independent, unafraid. With all the stresses of our lives during this time, the years have not been easy for him. I'm just now beginning to realize the toll it has taken on him. So many years that I was consumed with my healing, so many years I could not be there for him.

Good for David. I often think that he has pulled himself up and has managed to accomplish so much.

Beth has abdominal surgery tomorrow to eliminate old scars and ridges from four previous surgeries.

My echocardiogram is Friday. I go into the test with some trepidation. So many times I have received bad news, yet nothing major has occurred to raise the specter of doubt about my heart.

March 25, 1999

Beth woke up around noon, tired and groggy from the pain medication she was given to blunt the effects of abdominal surgery the day before. Steve said he would be home by lunchtime, but it wasn't unusual for him to be late, maybe even an hour or so. He had come to believe that time spent with his patients meant as much to their recovery as any prescription for medicines or referrals to specialists.

Around 1:30 P.M., the phone rang. It was Steve, calling on his cell phone. He had pulled off the Albuquerque downtown freeway on the Second Street exit. He was fifteen minutes from home. She didn't understand what he said at first. It was a strange way to begin a conversation.

"Are you going to be all right by yourself?" he said. "I don't think I can come home."

"Why not?" Beth said.

"My chest is on fire," he said.

She closed her eyes against the rush of fear.

"Steve, why are you calling me?" she said.

It was more plea than question.

"Call 911," she said.

"OK," he said. "I'll call 911."

She knew what this phone call meant. So did he. They had run out of miracles. He was somewhere in Albuquerque, calling from his car, his chest on fire, and they had no miracles left. They had talked about this moment, trying to prepare themselves for it. They had wondered how it would come.

"Steve, I love you," she said.

"I love you," he said.

They were the last words that passed between them.

She hung up the phone and checked the bedside clock. Steve needed time to make the 911 call. She waited five minutes before calling him back.

It had been almost five years since he was diagnosed with Takayasu's. He had undergone three heart surgeries. The experience brought fundamental changes to how he viewed the teaching and practice of his medical art. The disease brought stress that turned him inward, selfish and angry, then found him reaching out as he had never done in his life.

Just that morning, when Steve and David woke up long before the alarm clocks went off, Beth couldn't tell who was more excited about David's eleventh birthday—her youngest son, who had been refining his birthday wish list for six months, or her husband, who had been making the party arrangements, ordering the birthday cake, and breaking precedent by allowing David to open gifts early in the morning, as if late March might have brought a second Christmas.

She thought this departure from custom had been yet another product of Steve's awareness of time. If a moment of joy with his family presented itself, he saw no reason to delay its pleasure. He seized it. These moments were to be embraced at their first appearance, not postponed or relegated to secondary importance, especially now, when he didn't have the luxury of putting something off until tomorrow or even later today.

Steve and the boys had joked around all through the morning. Before he took them to school on his way to work, they all came in the bedroom to say good-bye to Beth and so David could show off his birthday gifts.

After making sure Beth had everything she would need close by on the night stand, Steve kissed her good-bye and left with the boys.

He dropped Andy off first, then went to a bagel shop to have breakfast with David, a departure from their customary McDonald's mornings. After taking David to school, he went to work at his family practice clinic. The morning went well. He performed a vasectomy, a welcome break from the routine. When he left, no one at the clinic saw any reason for worry.

After Steve's phone call, Beth got up and dressed. She took a pain pill because she knew she would be riding in a car to the hospital. She prayed.

Five minutes dragged by. She dialed his cell phone number. No answer.

She called their close friends, Brian and Brenda Kilcup. The Kilcups had been through this kind of thing with them six times. After the first time Steve was rushed to the emergency room, the families devised a plan in which Beth would call the Kilcups and they would alert everyone else on the phone list. It was always Brenda who made sure the Hsi children were taken care of and the house picked up and the pets fed.

No one answered the Kilcup phone. Beth left a message. When Brenda Kilcup's oldest daughter, Charmayne, came home shortly afterwards, she picked up the message and tracked down her parents to let them know Steve was in the emergency room. She told her parents later that she didn't know why, but she felt this time was different from the rest.

Twenty minutes passed before Beth's phone rang again. It was the emergency room physician, a close family friend and for years a Wednesday night volleyball player with Steve. He was on duty when the ambulance brought Steve to the hospital. He told Beth it didn't look good. Steve was in bad shape. The physician said he had already called his wife and that she would come by to drive Beth to the hospital.

Beth called Steve's parents and his brother.

An hour had passed from the time Steve called and when Beth arrived at the hospital. Walking into the emergency room, Beth thought it surreal, the landscape of a strange dream. In her long nursing career, she had worked in emergency rooms all over the country. She knew the people and the system, the controlled rush of code teams, the litter and debris piling up on the floor under a gurney when a code team tried to save a life—she knew it all intimately, and now it seemed unreal, an illusion.

Someone found a wheelchair for her and pushed her to the glass-enclosed room where the team worked on Steve. She caught a glimpse of his face, his eyes open, unseeing.

A team member came out to her.

"It's bad," he said.

As they prepared to take him to the catheter lab to test for damage to his heart, a nurse saw Beth nearby and motioned for the team to step away from the gurney in the hallway leading to the lab. Beth pushed herself from the wheelchair, stopping a moment to adjust her eyes from the glare of the emergency room's lights to the dimly lit hallway, and then she went to Steve.

She took his left hand in hers. It felt cold. She stroked the side of his head with her right hand, a gesture he had told her many times soothed him. She always did it when he was sick or afraid. Sometimes she did it when he slept. She bent down, whispered his name and told him she was there. He didn't respond.

The code team stood a few feet away, ghosts of her own long medical career, reminders of the times she stood where they now did. In their eyes she saw the sympathy and sorrow she had so often felt in the presence of her own dying patients and their families. She tried to reject the reason for their compassion. To acknowledge it was to acknowledge that Steve would not wake up. This time wouldn't be just another terrible scare, like all the others.

She kissed Steve's forehead and squeezed his hand. She looked up at a nurse and nodded. The team pushed the gurney through the double doors leading to the lab.

Friends started arriving at the emergency room. Brenda Kilcup's phone tree had worked well. Word spread quickly, just as it had done throughout the hospital. Steve practiced at Presbyterian; he underwent his first heart surgery there. People knew him.

His cardiologist, Dr. Paul Cochran, came out from the cath lab and went to Beth. He told her there wasn't much they could do. Steve had ruptured the juncture where the aorta was sewn in. There was nothing to save.

Despite its futility, the cardiologist and Beth talked about surgery. He asked Beth what she wanted to do and for a moment her medical knowledge and experience seemed a curse that denied her one last hope, even a false one.

"No surgery," she said. "I don't want to put him through that."

Steve was moved to the Cardiac Care Unit on the seventh floor. The nurses made him as comfortable as possible and then left the family alone. Steve's parents, his brother, Andy and his wife and children, came to the hospital. The TGIF group from the First Presbyterian Church came and soon all of them crowded into the CCU room.

Brenda Kilcup brought Steve's 13-year-old son, Andy; Steve's mother brought David, who had celebrated his eleventh birthday that morning. The boys stayed for a short time and then asked to leave. Beth told them it would be all right if they stayed. They declined. They said they couldn't watch him die.

Brenda Kilcup took them to her home to wait with her children and Steve's nephew and niece.

That evening, 9-year-old Kristen Salazar, the daughter of friends John and Marci Salazar, leaned over Steve's bed and kissed him on the cheek.

Steve shuddered and raised his head as if he were responding to her touch.

"Then he was gone," Beth said. "It was as if he waited until everybody got there."

Dr. Steven D. Hsi died at 8:43 P.M., March 25, 1999. He was 44 years old.